ACTION
LEARNING

ACTION
LEARNING

A Practitioner's Guide

Ian McGill and Liz Beaty

KOGAN
PAGE

First published in 1992

Kogan Page Limited
120 Pentonville Road
London N1 9JN

© Ian McGill and Liz Beaty, 1992

British Library Cataloguing in Publication Data

A CIP record for this book is available from the British Library.

ISBN 0 7494 0580 5

Typeset by DP Photosetting, Aylesbury,
Printed and bound in Great Britain by
Biddles Ltd, Guildford and King's Lynn

Contents

Acknowledgements

There are many whose help we wish to acknowledge, many more than we can name. In particular we wish to thank all those who have been set members in sets that we have facilitated over the period of the writing. We originally wanted to name them with their agreement. The number of people would have been extensive. To omit others would have been invidious. To all set members with whom we have worked we can only express our thanks for what we have learned through your contributions, struggles and development using action learning.

Our thanks to those who made action learning happen for staff and management development purposes in some of the organizations in which we have had the opportunity to engage as set advisers over the period. In particular we would like to thank Judi Clements, Mike Elbro, Judith Drury, Stella Jackson, Chloe Stallibrass.

Much of our work owes its origins and continuation to the creative and supportive culture at the University of Brighton Business School where we have done much of our formative work with independent sets, self-facilitated sets and the integration of action learning into mainstream courses. Tom Bourner, Mary Britton and Paul Frost were with us in those developments and are still treading new ground. Jon Bareham as Dean helped to ensure with other staff the conditions for action learning to take root.

We wish to thank those who have taken the time to contribute ideas and to read critically our drafts. To Anne Brockbank of the University of North London our considerable thanks for her ideas toward Chapters 9 and 10, and to Mike Sharples of the University of Sussex for his continued insights. Thanks to Bob Sang of the University of Brighton and the Open Learning Foundation for his reflections on the management development chapters and the final chapter. Tom Bourner put in substantial time on reading much of the material, particularly Parts I and II and the chapter on higher education. Susan Weil of the Office of Public Management took on the task of reading the whole final draft prior to publication. Our appreciation to Susan and those who gave us their support and encouragement. We take full responsibility for the outcomes.

Thanks to Helen Carley and Robert Jones at Kogan Page for working with our time schedules and having patience with our idiosyncrasies.

As authors we have enjoyed working together and developing our ideas as we wrote; we hope our enthusiasm comes over to readers.

Finally we would like to add a comment made recently by Jon Bareham:

> When I first came across the concept of action learning I had a degree of cynicism and hesitation. As both a participant in action learning sets and as an observer of the value of the process to others, I now believe the concentration on and support for the learning of the individual results in a speed and depth of learning and often 'cognitive leaps' which other processes do not engender.

Ian McGill, Liz Beaty
London and Brighton
September 1992

Chapter 1

Using the Guide

Action learning is a process of learning and reflection that happens with the support of a group or 'set' of colleagues working with real problems with the intention of getting things done. The participants in the group or 'set' each take forward an important issue with the support of the other members of the set. The process helps people to take an active stance toward life and helps overcome the tendency to be passive toward the pressures of life and work.

The guide is for users to practise action learning – the *how* and *doing* of action learning. There is much written at theoretical and descriptive levels and many examples of the practice of action learning sets. Our endeavour is to detail how action learning can be made accessible so that users can create and run action learning sets themselves with growing confidence. We set out the key procedures and skills that participants need to gain effectively from action learning. We review the potential of action learning for management development and show how it can be a significant vehicle for learning in higher education.

Users of the Guide

The guide is intended for people who want to use action learning. It is for those who wish to introduce the idea to their colleagues and for those who wish to take part in action learning for effective personal learning and development. The guide can be used to introduce the concepts and processes involved to new practitioners and as a manual for those who facilitate action learning. We use the term 'manager' frequently in the text. We use a very broad definition of managers as people who *take* responsibility for their lives and work. In this sense 'everyone a manager' enables all to think and act managerially (Boydell *et al*, 1991). This also means that within organizations all staff can be considered in terms of their developmental needs.

The guide is a practical contribution for individuals to engage in their personal development. By 'personal development' we mean how a person can reflect on their work and life (we prefer not to make a separation between work and the rest of our lives) with a view to making things happen or change. At a task level it may be tackling a problem like making better use of time or working through a project. At a more reflective level it may be whether to change the direction of a career or how to find the 'right' balance in life between competing interests.

Action learning in companies and the public and voluntary sectors

For organizations wanting to develop their staff, action learning sets provide a means of enabling that development to happen. The process combines a person's direct work experience with their learning as opposed to the traditional separation of direct work experience from learning associated with education. Being in-house, about real issues and continuous, a person's learning tends to be cumulative and relevant as opposed to off-site workshops and residentials that may not be geared to the individual's needs and where the fall-off in learning is known to be significant. Moreover, the action learning process develops and enhances skills and qualities that are required by organizations for their effective operation, contributing to the development of the organization as well as the individuals employed.

Our guide is addressed to those in industrial and service organizations (private, public and voluntary) who can influence and determine staff and management development policy and its implementation. The guide is for staff to use as a resource in securing their own development needs and enhancing their skills through participation in action learning sets.

Action learning in higher education

Higher education has traditionally been characterized by a clear separation from industry and service organizations. Characteristically, students get taught/learn in colleges and then go on to work following completion of the course with little linkage between the two worlds. Moreover, students of higher education have traditionally been taught didactically, 'one subject/ discipline' in lecture-receiving mode. The trend toward student-centred learning, transferable skills and closer links with industry and services has required higher education institutions to look to ways of linking with the 'outside' world and introducing more effective methods of student learning.

Action learning provides a method of enabling that learning as well as acquiring and enhancing a significant range of transferable skills.

In higher education at undergraduate and postgraduate levels the guide is useful to teaching staff, including course organizers, who wish to move toward alternative teaching and learning methods. Course designers and teaching staff can adopt the method, develop the skills, and use action learning sets as a primary mode of learning or as a supplement to other methods. Student learners can use the guide to enhance their practice in action learning sets.

Independent action learning sets

One of the liberating features of action learning for us has been the ability to create our own sets which were independent of the organizations in which we happened to be employed. Indeed our experience of independent sets has been one of the motives in compiling this guide. Independent sets can be self-facilitated by the members; alternatively the set can be facilitated by a set adviser who has the skills to get the set up and running. Once the set members have acquired the skills the set adviser withdraws.

We found that the support and challenge of a set met many of our needs for our own personal development. We could share the struggle of learning and grappling with change which otherwise we do in isolation from others and without the feedback of others. Realizing that we need not be on our own in whatever our struggle gave us a strong commitment to action learning.

Colleagues, friends and students can therefore use the guide to set up their own action learning sets.

Action learning for trainers and developers

Trainers, consultants and developers may also find our guide useful to extend their repertoire as professional practitioners and advocates of effective development using action learning as the method of development.

How the Guide is Organized

We seek to enable people to benefit from *using* the guide to *do* action learning as opposed to simply reading about action learning. The organization of the chapters reflects that purpose.

Part I, Doing Action Learning, Chapters 2 to 7, conveys detailed descriptions of the practice of action learning for those who wish to be effective set members and for those who facilitate action learning. These chapters are intended for readers to become familiar with the method and feel confident about *doing* action learning.

Chapter 2 sets out what action learning is and how it works. The aim is to de-mystify the term, encourage the use of action learning and to explain how to organize and run sets. Chapter 3 introduces different types of action learning, how it can be used as a training and development vehicle in organizations, in higher education, and outside organizations amongst friends and colleagues. Chapter 4 defines how a set works once the set has formed. Set meetings are put into the context of the action which a set member takes between set meetings. In this chapter we describe the basic procedures of the set – what to do and when – and examine in more detail the processes of set meetings – the *how* of action learning set meetings. It is important that the set reflects on its processes: how the set is working, what is happening below the surface. An examination of the process, as opposed to what is being discussed (a set member's issues or content) deals with how individual set members are feeling and how the whole set is working. Chapter 5 examines how to be an effective set member from three perspectives: as a set member receiving support; as a set member giving support to another member who is addressing her/his issue; and finally as part of the whole set. Facilitators, when to use them, their role and qualities forms the basis of Chapter 6. Here we examine how the skills and qualities needed by facilitators are acquired and enhanced. This chapter is useful for set members as it may help them 'model' their own set practice on the facilitator for, in a sense, all members of the set are facilitators. Further, facilitators should, in our view, be aiming to make themselves redundant as the set becomes self-facilitating and independent of the facilitator. Some sets may start as self-facilitated sets. Chapter 7 is for potential set members to check out the *how* of self-facilitation.

Part II, Developing Action Learning Skills, Chapters 8 to 10, introduces the skills used for effective action learning. Given support for the idea of action learning, how is it introduced to potential users? To obtain a real sense of what action learning will be like it is insufficient merely to describe it in words. Chapter 8 shows how action learning can be introduced to potential users by doing it. The chapter provides a workshop format for the person introducing it and details how to design and run the workshop. The workshop conveys to participants an understanding of what it would feel like to be in a set. Once participants agree to become part of a set they enter the formation stage which is usually the first meeting. This is the stage when participants really decide to continue. Membership of the set must be voluntary to ensure real commitment.

There are a number of basic (but sophisticated) skills that we bring to all interpersonal situations. An action learning set places significant emphasis on some of these. Examples include our skills of listening, reflecting back, disclosure, empathy, giving and receiving feedback, questioning and specifying actions. The aim of Chapters 9 and 10 is to make the skills required for effective set membership more explicit and to enable potential set members to reflect on and enhance their own skills.

In Part III, The Uses of Action Learning, the main emphases are the uses of action learning for management development, as a contribution to learning in higher education and the features in the guide that we consider take action learning forward. In Chapters 11 and 12 we consider how action learning can contribute to management development in organizations in terms of relevance and the development of the whole person. This fits with the trend of ensuring that employees can be adaptive in their own interests as well as that of the employer. We go further in these chapters to show how action learning can contribute to the systems for management development, organizational learning and the emerging notion of the learning company (Pedler *et al*, 1991).

In Chapter 13 we examine how action learning can be used in higher education: as an effective means of enabling and enhancing transferable skills and learning to learn into course development and delivery; to provide more flexible teaching/learning methods; as a basis for greater interaction with industry and the service sector.

Finally, in Chapter 14 we examine the features of the guide that we consider take action learning forward and extend its use in contributing to individual, organizational and social change.

Routes Through the Guide

People will have different purposes in using the guide. We do not intend that the guide be taken in at one reading from page one onwards. We have included a glossary for users unfamiliar with action learning. We suggest some routes, depending upon the intention, role and background of the user, as:

- a potential set member intending to join an action learning set – Chapters 2, 4, 5 and later 9 and 10

- an existing set member wishing to reflect upon and enhance their experience of sets – 3, 5, 6, 7, 9, 10 and Part II, 11 and 12 and/or 13, 14
- set members with some experience of action learning on participating in self-facilitated and possibly independent sets – 3, 6, 7, 9, 10 and 14
- facilitators of sets – 6, 9, 10 and 8
- management developers, human resource development specialists and managers with responsibility for action learning with:
  - some knowledge and experience of action learning – 3, 11, 12, 14 and 8
  - little knowledge and experience of action learning – 2, 3, 4, 6, 11, 12, 14 and 8
- course organizers, developers in higher education with:
  - some knowledge and experience of action learning – 3, 5, 6, 13, 14, 8, 9 and 10
  - little knowledge and experience of action learning – 2, 3, 4, 13, 5, 6, 7, 8, 9 and 10

Where We are Coming From

We are writing this guide as enthusiastic practitioners of action learning. We work as facilitators of sets or as set members, and our development has benefited from both. We work in the public and private sector and in higher education using action learning as a major vehicle for development and change in individuals and organizations. In contributing to making action learning more accessible we also wish to encourage more experimentation with its use, both in terms of ways of enabling people to develop and learn and to serve a range of purposes in and outside organizations.

We work with women and men. The text reflects this with examples that are gender-specific rather than attempting a neutral and genderless language.

Our collaboration in writing this guide comes from our shared belief and experience in the methods and benefits of action learning sets which can be dramatic, leading to lasting, effective and productive learning. Finally, we cannot omit the contribution of Reg Revans (1980; 1983) to the initial creation of the idea of action learning and its long advocacy over years in conditions where few people could understand its potential. The conditions for its use now appear to be more fruitful due, in part, to his tenacity.

DOING ACTION LEARNING

Chapter 2

What is Action Learning and How Does it Work?

Action learning is a continuous process of learning and reflection, supported by colleagues, with an intention of getting things done. Through action learning individuals learn with and from each other by working on real problems and reflecting on their own experiences. The process helps us to take an active stance towards life and helps to overcome the tendency to think, feel and be passive towards the pressures of life.

Action learning is based on the relationship between reflection and action. We all learn through experience by thinking through past events, seeking ideas that make sense of the event and help us to find new ways of behaving in similar situations in the future. This thinking through or reflection is the essential link between past action and more effective future action. In our everyday lives, however, we do not always find time for reflection. It is easy just to let things happen and respond to the demands of our lives without much thought of our own part in it. In times of crisis or radical change reflection becomes more important and also more difficult: it is at these times that we make powerful decisions about our future. Action learning builds on this normal human process of learning, making the links more clearly in order to make them effective. We believe that reflection is a necessary precursor to effective action and that learning from experience can be enhanced through deliberate attention to this relationship.

Action learning involves a group of people (called a set) working together for a concentrated period of time. We know that making powerful decisions is greatly enhanced by working with others. The focus, however, is essentially on the individual. It is the individual who comes to the set to learn from experience and to move on to more effective action. The set enables this process to take place through concentrated group effort focused on the issues of each individual.

When I join a set other people help me to understand my situation; to explore issues and pressures around me and help me to form a sound judgement about my future action. It remains for me to decide how to act or to decide not to act as a result of this work in the set. With action learning I can be more powerful by bringing to conscious awareness feelings and reflections on my past and current situation which can usefully inform my next action. The members of my set will help me to do this by supporting my reflections and challenging my assumptions. The action that I decide as a result of this will be clearer, better informed and more likely to be undertaken.

In this book we describe action learning as a process; a powerful vehicle for development which has the potential for wide and varied use. The most common use has been in management development where managers have used the process to work on organizationally based projects and in doing so have developed themselves as managers as well as benefiting the organization. The power to link effective action with the development of the person who undertakes the action makes action learning useful in many other areas. Recently the management development potential has been seen by those teaching in higher education and an increasing number of courses are using action learning. The integration of action learning into courses has enhanced the linking of the academic world of theory to the practical world of work and so is becoming popular for part-time management development courses. More recently still this idea has been transferred to other courses of professional development, eg a course of professional training for teachers in higher education and even into undergraduate programmes to support project work. We have also used action learning less formally as a support for colleagues who want to develop themselves at the same time as working on particular projects. Examples of the use of action learning and its relationship to learning and development are given in Part III of this book.

Why Use the Term 'Action Learning'?

The term 'action learning' says it all: learning through action. 'Action' because the group is more than a simple support group; each member takes action on their own issue after reflection with the group. 'Learning' because the opportunity to reflect on experience with the support of others followed by action means that set members engage in learning from experience in order to change rather than simply repeating previous patterns. The essential point is that action learning is an intentional strategy based on normal, but unusual, effective practice. If, for example, I really am stuck and don't know what to do, I will seek out a trusted friend or colleague to discuss what I could do. The people who help me most will usually not attempt to tell me what I should do but rather listen attentively and help me to find my own way towards a next step. This is what I need in order to act decisively and in a way which will take me forward. Sometimes I feel that to ask for this quality of attention is an imposition even though I will be able to reciprocate at another time. The joy of action learning in sets is the feeling of helping as much as receiving help – in the same session. It also allows me to explore this way of learning from experience for less crucial events, making it part of my normal approach to life rather than kept only for times of crisis. It also legitimates something rare in normal interaction – a situation where a group of people focus all their attention on supporting one person. The times I have asked for help from a trusted friend have been one-to-one interactions or a series of one-to-one interactions. A set is an efficient way of accelerating this kind of support.

Often in describing the basic process to colleagues they say, 'Ah yes! We do that all the time'. It is useful to talk through ideas and reflect with other people – why use jargon? On closer examination the difference is usually in the intentional nature of the set. Set members have joined together expressly to work on a project, issue or problem which they intend to undertake, progress or solve. Furthermore the set members intend to learn from this process in order to develop personally and/or professionally. People will often reflect on past actions and next steps with friends or colleagues and can learn from doing so. With action learning it is the learning through action and reflection that is the reason for meeting. It is the legitimacy and formalization of these events over an extended period of time with a consistent group membership that makes it special. The intention to act as a result of the learning is the rationale for the group discussion rather than a by-product of it. The action learning set meetings end with each individual having clear and specific action points which they have committed themselves to as a result of the meeting.

What is the Nature of an Action Learning Project?

Action learning is based on individuals learning from experience through reflection and action. The action side of the equation is called a project. An action learning project can be anything that a set member wishes to work on with the aid of the set process. Projects can be specific issues or problems; they can be clearly specified or complex and messy. The important thing is that the project is not one where the end point and the stages in between are clearly mapped out in advance – in this case the set would be of little help to the presenter of the project unless time and motivation were to be the issues brought to the set. Other projects that would benefit little from action learning are ones that are really only puzzles which have a right or wrong answer and all the set member needs is the answer. Joining a set is unlikely to be the most efficient way of getting the answer.

Projects do not have to start when the set begins and finish as the set ends: there might be a one-to-one correspondence between a project and the life of a set but this is rare. We have found that usually the project which a set member brings to the set has pre-dated the action learning set and often continues after the set has completed its cycle. Sometimes a member's project ends before the negotiated end-point of a set and here the set member might choose to bring another project to the set in order to maintain the membership until the agreed ending.

Projects have to be real and alive. That is, they should not be manufactured simply for the set – action learning is for enabling people to undertake action to further real issues or resolve real problems; it is not an artificial game to produce learning outside of experience. Set members also need to have some motivation in relation to the project, ie, they must want to do something about the issue or problem; they must be prepared to act – the set process is intended to empower. If a set member has no intention to further the project then the action learning process will be sterile.

In this book we use the term 'presenter' when we are referring to the set member as they bring their project to the set. The presenter does not 'do' the project in the set meeting, nor do they (necessarily) involve the other set members in any project-related task. The set meeting is the vehicle for reflection on actions in relation to the project and learning from the experience of that action. It is also the opportunity for deciding on the next actions to take.

How is an Action Learning Set Different from Other Types of Group?

The essence of an action learning set is its focus on the individual and their future action. The set has a basic design which is the 'one at a time' rule which produces a very different experience from working in many other types of group.

It is not like a seminar where a presentation is made on the basis of well-prepared material for a discussion by the group as a whole. Seminar papers are concerned with the world 'out there' but action learning sets are interested in the world out there as it is related to the individual set member and their particular context. Another difference is the lack of spontaneity in a seminar and the rules of discussion which are rarely focused on helping the individual who gave the seminar paper and still less based on action as a result of the discussion.

A set is not a team because a team has a well-defined group task whereas a set works on the action of individuals. A team must work for the benefit of the task they have to complete; they may care for each other but their rationale for being together is in order to work on a task. The rationale for a set to be together is to work on the future action of each individual set member. If the set members shared a project they could work as a team as well as a set. Here the set structure would not be appropriate for every meeting of the team. The team would need to meet to undertake some of the actions that had been decided at the set meeting that involved the whole or part of the team working together. The main function of the set in a group project would remain, however, enabling each individual to progress with the project for him or herself.

Sets are not like formal meetings; they do not have a role for a chair or an agenda. Sets do not have free-flowing discussion or debate aimed at involving everyone in decision-making and they certainly do not have votes to decide on future action. The flow of set discussion is based around the presenter's issue and their need for support and challenge. The set may mirror formal meetings in having tight time constraints and in producing minutes, but the minutes of set meetings are simply the action points agreed and do not contain a record of the discussion.

A set is more than a support group because although set members are there to support each individual in moving forward with their issue they are also there to challenge and can take a more assertive role. The focus is on the learning from the actions taken with the aim of strengthening the individual as well as in getting things done. The supporting that is done leaves responsibility firmly with the presenter.

A set is not a counselling group. A set member presenting their issue to the set can expect to be listened to and to have questions and comments aimed at helping them but they should not expect counselling, and this is not what is on offer. Set members can find action learning a conducive environment to explore personal problems and discover underlying personal issues but they are unlikely to find, in the set, the therapy they might need to deal with psychological problems.

A set is also distinct from a self-development group in its concern with, and attention to, action. The set is concerned less with self-discovery and more with acting on the learning gained from reflection on experiences. The focus is on making a difference in the outer world, although the inner world is inevitably involved in the process of reflection.

Who can be Set Members?

The obvious but trite answer here is 'anyone and everyone', but this is less helpful than attempting to delimit the service that action learning affords. The best way to explore the limits of action learning is through examples. We have used action learning work-based sets for management development. Sets have been introduced as part of academic programmes of study for part-time students who have a professional role and for full-time students to support their project work. We have used it in training teachers. We have also used action learning sets in supporting change within organizations. We have ourselves been members of sets which are voluntary groups working within an organization but for the primary benefit of the staff rather than organization. The uses are many and divergent and therefore membership is likewise varied. These examples are illustrated and described more fully in Chapters 12 and 13.

Another way to describe who can be a member of a set is to say, 'anyone who can benefit from the experience'. This might be anticipated by someone reading through the values underpinning the process and asking themselves if they would like to take part. People who started off sceptical have become ardent followers of the process but also some who try it have found that the process is not what they required at the time. The best way to find out about action learning is to do it.

Who is the Set For?

The set is for the people within it. The focus of the action learning process is on individually based learning from action, which leads to development for the individual, and for their organization, through the project. Having made this point, however, we want now to qualify it. Working through action learning sets can have influence beyond the people immediately involved. The people who work closely with the set members will surely notice the difference in their demeanour and their ability to get things done. Over time they are likely to witness an individual with increased confidence and ability to respond and work through change. Depending on the focus of the project, they may witness a surge of energy and thoughtful activity that transforms the working context. If many people within the organization take part in the action learning sets, the organization itself may change. Not only do working arrangements and interpersonal relationships benefit from the projects and the increased empathy of the people but the people who make up the organization learn to manage the organization in a new way. They learn about the process of action learning which is transferable out of the set and into life in general. In short, where action learning becomes a feature of the organization itself, the organization takes on some of the features of a 'Learning Company' (Pedler *et al*, 1991).

An organization investing in its people through the provision of action learning programmes will find that it gains more than projects – it will receive as interest on its investment, developed individuals and development of the organization itself. There must, however, be a personal pay-off for individuals. If the organization wishes to keep a tight control over the content of work within sets, the set may become impotent; set members will feel constrained to explore only the obvious and visible aspects of problems and issues rather than their bases. If this kind of control is required, other processes such as quality circles might be more appropriate. It is important that the set members have the support of their organization where they have clients for their projects. Negotiation of the original brief for the sets and for each individual project is essential. One company which has made use of action learning for its staff through a programme of study had this to say about its results:

> The action learning programme has been a cornerstone of our management development. The company has gained a trained management workforce but the time away from work has been justified as much for the work done for the company during that time as for the resulting development of its people. The projects have had real effects although they were originally designed primarily to be vehicles for learning. (Comment from a client/sponsor of a student on an action learning programme)

One department in local government included the following statements from participants in its review of the process:

> It gave me peace of mind knowing that there is a date in my diary when I can raise matters with my colleagues.

> Where problems threatened to undermine my confidence often the set helped to empower me again.

> In the past twelve months I have made more progress than in the previous three years in the job and much has to do with my participation in the set.

> Learning to work better in a group has carried over in other group situations in my work and having greater confidence to speak, but also to listen. (Extracts from review document.)

What Problems/Issues can Members Bring to a Set?

One answer to this question is 'anything'; however, there are some projects and some issues that would be helped very little by work through a set. Very trivial questions are unworthy of set time and problems that are outside my own authority to act upon are rather pointless projects for action learning. However my feelings about my lack of authority to act, and what to do about it, may be an excellent project. It is worth remembering when choosing a subject that I will be likely to learn more if the issue or project is important to me. Another likelihood is that the shape of the project or the way I describe it at the beginning of the set process is unlikely to be the way I describe it by the end. Most people find that the project transforms under the scrutiny of the set:

> What I thought was my problem turned out to be something else entirely – the set

helped me to uncover layers upon layers until I hit upon the real issue – I would not have been able to describe this to anyone at the beginning.

The set process is different for different people. Some people spend a great deal of set time reflecting on their experience while others concentrate more on planning the next action. The balance can change from one set meeting to another so that on some occasions I may not have very much time at all to decide on my action plan while on others I spend the whole session in formulating it.

People also differ in their focus, some being very keen to explore the environment around them, the context they are in and the effects of different types of action, while other people are more at home describing the inner world of their feelings and thoughts in trying to understand themselves. Whichever is the main focus, the role of the other set members is to facilitate this so that the reflection can be effective in generating an action plan. Set members may also wish at times to challenge the focus being taken by the presenter. Thus if the presenter has spent all their time discussing the project in relation to the objective world 'out there', it would be of service to ask a question focusing on the inner world of feelings and vice versa. The focus on task and process is a continuum which can be usefully distinguished and explored separately in set meetings.

Life Span of a Set

Sets need some time to work properly. Because of the cycle of action and reflection, sets feed on the work that goes on in between the set meetings. The life of the set depends a great deal on the nature of the projects that individual set members bring and the frequency of set meetings. The set's life is complete when the individuals have gained all they can from the set with regard to the project they brought to it. This is complicated somewhat by the fact that projects are unlikely to end all at the same time. We have found that although sets vary in their life span, from six months to three years, there is usually a need for a clear initial commitment for a certain number of meetings and that reviewing after these has extended the set's life by general agreement or signalled the end of the set. In our experience there is generally an easy consensus on this issue. Where a minority of set members want a set for longer than others there is often the possibility of joining another existing set or forming a new one. The key word here is flexibility. The set works for as long as the members feel that it is helping them to progress. At some point the members will have completed the projects that they brought to the set and will either decide to remain in the set and bring another issue or to draw the set process to a close.

It is possible to get hooked on action learning. Both of us have rarely been without a set (as members not facilitators) since we first began working in this way and this is not rare. Many people who have been in sets we have facilitated have gone on to work in other sets or have started up new sets of their own. We believe that this cascade is a testimony to the effectiveness of the action learning process.

Underpinning Action Learning

Experiential learning cycle

The most important aspect of action learning is the relationship between action and learning. We can learn about the world and about ourselves through reflection on past action. We can construct our future action from our reflections on our learning. Kolb described this as a cycle of experiential learning, as shown in Figure 2.1.

Belief in the power of the experiential learning cycle is at the heart of our investment in action learning as a method for professional and personal development. The stages of reflection and generalization are undertaken with the help of the set. The presenter also designs their next action at the end of their time and then undertakes this action in the testing stage and experiences the results in order to bring this to further reflection and generalization in the next set meeting. The cycle continues until the issue is resolved and the

Figure 2.1 *The Kolb learning cycle*

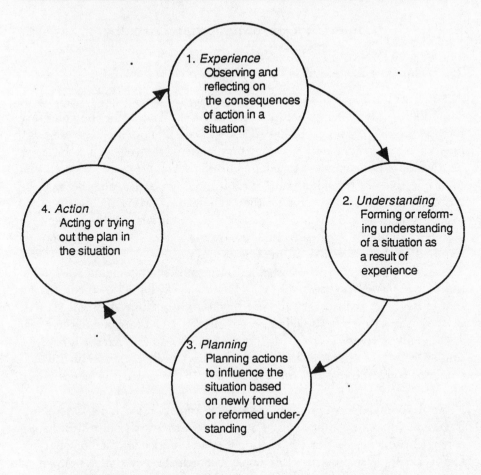

Figure 2.2 *The learning process* (Pedler et al, 1986)

learning complete for the time being. A corresponding stage view of this process has been captured by Pedler *et al* (1986) (see Figure 2.2).

Observing, reflecting on experience, leads to making sense of that experience in a new way, leading to understanding. Understanding can lead to insights which allow for new plans, new strategies for action and new modes of behaviour. These plans lead to new actions which have an effect in the context which lead to experience which can be as expected or have consequences quite different from those expected. This leads on through another evaluative cycle with reflection and learning occurring at each stage.

Values Underpinning Action Learning

The voluntary nature of set membership

Action learning is a voluntary endeavour. Being a member of a set cannot be compulsory. Membership cannot be imposed. The value of voluntary membership of sets underpins our book. We commend action learning as a form of management and personal development as well as a vehicle for organizational learning and development. However, we take as a given that to be effective for individuals and organizations action learning needs to be based on the fundamental value that joining in, starting, being in and if necessary leaving a set is a decision for the person who wishes to be a set member. Similarly, a person who takes on the role of set adviser cannot be required or obliged to take on the role.

A willing set member who wishes to get the most out of the time devoted to the set meeting will be *with* the set in an attentive way for her own benefit and that of the other members of the set. Involuntary membership will act as a block on the set member's willingness to engage in the working of the set. If a set member attends because she has been told to do so, then she is likely to display feelings of resentment or perhaps attempt to hide such feelings which would be conveyed in other ways. This can only be destructive of the group and its work.

We devote Chapter 8 to getting started with action learning. One of our intentions in writing that chapter is to enable those who are introducing action learning to give potential action learners an idea and feel of what it is like to do it. We also trust this book will help to make action learning accessible and easy to use.

Potential set members may come to action learning with some scepticism. That is different from hostility arising from imposition. A sceptical potential set member may have some of the same thoughts, feelings and questions. The solution is to provide the means for thoughts, feelings and questions to be addressed. *Describing* how action learning works may allay some of the concerns. *Doing* introductory sessions which defer commitment to the set is probably more helpful as this conveys a much fuller picture.

Commitment follows from the voluntary value. Set members once voluntarily wishing to be in the set develop a commitment to it. This means displaying in behaviour and actions a willingness to give some priority to set meetings and to be prepared to offer to other set members that degree of attention required to make the process work. In return for this commitment the set member will receive that quality of attention from other members when discussing her issue.

Action learning and a positive approach to life

Action learning is the antithesis of believing that we can do nothing about our situation. Whatever the context, people who use action learning believe that there is always something, however small, that can be done or positively not done. Believing that something can be done is not the same as saying that everything is under our control and still less that all problems are our fault. It does mean, however, that it is our responsibility first of all to review the situation and the context and to identify our own position and ability to manoeuvre within the situation. Very often our tendency is to blame others for things we don't like about our situation and therefore to stop thinking about our responsibility for our own problems. In using action learning I ask myself fundamental questions – what do I want to happen? What can I do to move towards this as an outcome? What can I do to cope with the situation in the meantime? Somewhat surprisingly, there is always something that I can do and in thinking through the issues involved I become clearer about my own contribution to the situation as presently constructed. Identifying what action it is possible to take also means that I may decide to take no action. This is an important point. The cycle of reflection on past action and present situation may reveal to me that the best thing to do next is *nothing*. In action learning there are usually three stages to go through: identification of the problem, identification of possible actions, identification of the specific action I want to take. I can at least make one person's worth of difference to the world.

Reflection is a key to learning from experience

Action learning is a process which adds structure to our experience by giving a set amount of time to reflection. The action learning set's two main functions are: to support individuals in reflecting on their past action in order to learn from experience; and to explore their current issue, concern or problem in order to help in the construction of the next actions. In both of these functions the quality of the reflection is the key to success. Reflection on past actions makes the difference between having 20 years of experience and having one year of experience 20 times.

With action learning, reflection in sets allows for a much greater level of awareness of the complexity of the internal and external world and their interrelationships through the support, challenge and empathy of the members of the set. The fact that I belong to a set which meets once a month means that I will spend time on reflection both at the set meetings and in preparation of them. The regularity of the set puts my issues higher on my list of priorities and means that I make an implicit (and sometimes formally written) contract to work on the issue, ie to take action in relation to it. Just the time allocation itself helps but the spur of peer pressure within the process of the set meeting is also an important motivator (cf voluntary nature). The structure of the set meeting with its focus on individuals gives a focus to my issue that I can't duck and the action points which I decide on at the end of my time adds an imperative to act on my reflections. Action learning is an effective way of making the cycle of action and reflection work.

No one is more expert than the presenter on her issue

The underlying principle in action learning sets is that the individual is and remains responsible for his or her own problem, issue or concern. In joining the set she or he can expect to find help in dealing with these things but cannot expect that anyone else will tell her what to do or solve his problem for him. In fact to be successful the set need not be made up of people who know each other, nor do they need to understand the context within which the others work. This knowledge is often irrelevant. The main function of set members is not to offer advice (although this has its place at times) but rather to help each individual to understand their situation better by exploration through reflection and to challenge assumptions underlying these reflections in order to decide the best course of future action. The information the individual has about his issue made up from his own view of the situation, his feelings about it and his knowledge of its context is fuller and more complex than any other individual could possibly have.

In an important sense the individual with the problem is the only person who really has access to the information needed to answer the fundamental questions: Why is this issue important to me? What do I feel about the situation? What happened the last time I acted in relation to it? What did that feel like? What do I believe could happen next? and so on .... This information is the data that the set works with to help the individual explore their issue, to learn from their experience and to formulate and plan new actions. The individual is truly the world expert in their own issue.

Support and challenge

We believe that support and challenge lie at the heart of the set member's role. Our development takes courage and in order to develop we need the support of others. Support can be offered in many different ways and the support offered by set members does not consist of taking over the doing of the project. No set member will volunteer to do my work for me but they will listen as I talk through what I want to do and the difficulties facing me. They will offer support through asking me questions that help me to explore the issues involved and through making suggestions about other angles I could explore. Support alone, however, may not be enough. It may produce a rather cosy atmosphere where I will not be spurred into action. The other aspect of the set member role is to challenge – to challenge my assumptions and my perspective – even to play devil's advocate and ask the uncomfortable 'what if' type of question. This challenging is not aggressive but rather supports my resolution into action and makes sure that the actions I choose have been reflected on as much as the problems that generated the need.

Sometimes the most supporting and the most challenging thing to say is nothing!

Empathy

At the centre of the set process is empathy. By empathy we mean the understanding of the position, context and emotional state of other set members. In order to know how best to enable the presenter to move forward with his project/problem or issue, I need to know what it feels like to be him right now. The more deep and full is my understanding, the more easily I can find the right words to enable him to progress. Empathy is not something that comes easily to most people and yet it is so useful in so many situations. Learning how to use empathy within a set can be one of the most important developmental experiences from the action learning process itself while guaranteeing a productive experience for the set as a whole. Empathy is described and discussed in some depth in Chapter 10.

Empowerment

Action learning is or should be easily accessible to most people. It is not a mysterious process which requires years of training. It has a clear structure and exists to serve a clear philosophy of learning – that which states that learning from experience requires reflection and action. We believe that action learning is of use far beyond its present boundaries and that it offers a democratic, liberating experience of learning to those who would try it. We also believe that it has great potential for developing organizations through harnessing the commitment of the people within the organization. By working in depth with individuals on organizational issues, the organization and the individual develop concurrently. The individual is empowered through being responsible for their own project while being supported throughout by the other set members. Action learning is empowering because it starts and ends with the individual and their project, making a necessary and direct link between thought and behaviour, theory and practice, reflection and action.

Quality of attention

Being a member of an action learning set takes a certain degree of commitment. Each member can gain a great deal for themselves from the work of the set but in return they commit to the set their attendance and good quality attention. In ordinary meetings we may attend selectively by focusing on issues of importance to us, relaxing our attention at other times when we are less concerned with the issue under discussion. In sets we attempt to give our whole attention to the presenter although the issue may be nothing whatsoever to do with us or to our advantage. This makes set working very different from our usual mode of operation and takes effort. The rewards are, however, very appealing. Having five people put all their attention at my disposal for 30 minutes can be an overwhelmingly powerful event. The quality of my set time as presenter will be directly responsive to the quality of attention I am given by the other set members. If a spirit of giving is engendered in the set all the members gain.

Trust and confidentiality

For a set to work well there needs to be a feeling of security for all the participants. Friends and colleagues learn to trust each other over time and in a set this will also be the case. However, confidentiality is a ground rule at the basis of an effectively working set. Only when there is complete confidence in this can a member truly explore their feelings and possible future actions. An action learning set holds the potential for real development for an individual and this will be enhanced through an open environment where an individual feels that what they say will not be held against them in the future. For the time of a set meeting other relationships are put aside and the set helps the individual in their own terms, keeping their own agendas in relation to the topic firmly to one side. This is not to ignore the consequences; a presenter could be usefully challenged by the perspective of someone who might be directly or indirectly affected by a future action. The set members, however, undertake to keep the set discussions and action points confidential to the set.

Development takes time

What is at stake in action learning is not simply more effective action. The more important and longer-lasting outcome is development for the individuals. Development does not happen overnight nor is it necessarily painless but it is worth striving for. Action learning is a form of accelerated learning where reflection is aided by others who focus for a time on the individual and their issues. Action learning deliberately lasts over a number of set meetings. The 'projects' that members are working on take time to develop. In looking at expected outcomes from an action and then after the event exploring the results of that action, real learning can result. The individual has feedback of a direct kind and also indirectly through the perspectives of other set members. Over a cycle which which typically lasts for a number of months, the set members learn about their ability to affect their environment and their ability to change themselves. Development like this takes time and it also requires confidence. The support of the set can generate in individuals the confidence to act in ways that on their own they would have been unable to contemplate. The action will be better thought through and therefore is likely to be more effective. Effective action brings its own rewards, not least in boosting confidence. This cycle of action, positive feedback from success and raised confidence is the key to development for an individual: confidence is a prerequisite to developing competence and being able to manage others and being more competent feeds back into a raised level of confidence.

An holistic approach

Action learning is based on valuing the whole person. By this we mean that the process involves taking into account the thoughts and feelings of the individual as well as the tangible results of their actions. The process of action learning is intentionally iterative between the objective world of things and subjective world of feelings and works on making explicit links between them. In the set the focus is on the subjective – the thoughts and feelings of the individual towards the world and how they are experiencing it. In between the set meetings the focus is on action, inaction (ie, deciding not to act) and the environmental responses to this action. In the action learning set meetings links are made between the past, the present and the future through the processes of reflection, attention to feelings and action planning. Feelings are important because they give us feedback which helps in making sense of our thoughts. The simple question 'What did you feel when that happened', or 'What do you feel about that now' are excellent in exploration of the last events in relation to the project and they tell us different things from questions about thoughts. The action learning process engages both thoughts and feelings in moving towards a plan for action.

This chapter has introduced our view of action learning and its potential for much wider use. The following chapters unpack this further with an emphasis on practical aspects of action learning.

Chapter 3

Types of Action Learning Sets

We distinguish between sets that are initiated and supported within an organization and sets that are initiated by colleagues in, out of or across organizations without the support of the latter. We have the following possibilities all of which will have some differences in the way sets are run and maintained:

- Sets sponsored by the organization
  a) with set advisers
  b) self-facilitated

In this category we include sets formed for management development purposes in an organization and those which are increasingly to be found in the educational context as part of a diploma, degree or postgraduate programme.

- Independent action learning sets
  a) with set advisers
  b) self-facilitated

These can be found within organizations or across organizations or organizationally free. They are formed by the participants themselves with their own personal and management development aims.

Sets that are self-facilitated are categorized under both headings in order to convey that action learning does not necessarily depend on a facilitator/set adviser. For the next section it will be assumed that sets have the support of a set adviser. Self-facilitated sets are considered in Chapter 7.

Sets Sponsored by the Organization

Taking initiative and gaining commitment for action learning

Two groups of people may initiate action learning within an organization. The first group are those who have responsibility for development and wish to use action learning as an important means of enabling staff and management development to happen. The second group are the people who wish to be participants in sets for their personal and management development. Both groups of people have responsibilities for ensuring that the sets are created and maintained.

The key here is the source of influence for initiating the creation of sets. For organizational support, particularly where resources in the form of time, finance and project initiatives are required, there is a need for a champion placed in the organization to make the action learning happen. The champion may be a managing director, head of staff/management development, trainer or someone who is an enthusiast to make action learning happen. Ideally the champion will be familiar with the use and effectiveness of action learning, what it is like to do action learning and the personal/managerial and organizational benefits.

Determining the issues brought to the set

We discuss particular applications of action learning in organizations in Chapters 11 and 12. Here we consider the basic approaches organizations may take to how they expect participant managers and staff to use sets.

The continuum in Figure 3.1 can be used to describe the range of ways in which sets can be used by set members. With organizationally sponsored sets it is important that there is clarity for the sponsors, set members and facilitators (in facilitated sets) as to which end of the continuum sets are expected to work.

The person responsible for initiating action learning can take a stance along

Figure 3.1 *Organizationally sponsored set continuum*

the continuum. Let's refer to him as the 'development manager'. At the left end of the continuum the organization, via the development manager, determines the parameters of a project in negotiation with the set member, 'client' (considered below) and a set adviser. There is shared 'ownership', between the set member and the organization, of the project and accountability by the set member is maintained mainly through the project. At the personal end of the continuum the set member is left to determine the issues she brings to the set with responsibility resting more with the set member to utilize the set for her development and with accountability resting more on the outcomes for their development in reflection with her line manager and the management developer responsible for creating the sets.

The organizational project

At the organization project end of the continuum the development manager will require staff joining sets to undertake a project that is directly geared to the needs of the organization. The member of staff joins a set to enable her to gain support whilst undertaking the project that has direct pay-offs for the organization. The project may be directly geared to the organization's strategic purposes or be a one-off problem-centred issue for resolution. The project could be based on an operational or a developmental problem. An operational problem would be one that concerned the existing way in which a product is produced or a service delivered which gets translated into a project to resolve or at least reduce the incidence of the problem. Examples may include:

- low morale in a front-line customer service department of an organization;
- reducing the number of return visits of clients to an organization by dealing with their needs more effectively first time.

A developmental issue or problem would be one which takes the organization and its members beyond the operational into new pathways of potential action:

- implementing a management development system;
- planning and implementing a monitoring strategy to reflect an equal opportunities policy;
- developing and implementing a new marketing strategy;
- introducing performance measurement into customer care programmes;
- identification, design and implementation of a staff development policy.

Enabling management development through project work via action learning sets has a two crucial aspects.

First, the problem tackled must be one for which there is not a prescribed solution. If we know how the problem is to be resolved it is not a problem. We just need to get on with it. However, I may have a problem doing it. This is a different matter. I may have a problem in undertaking the task I am addressing. An example would be where I lack the confidence to do a particular task. We will address this below at the personal development end of the continuum. An organization, in agreeing an organizational problem for resolution through a project, will want the project to be one that is at least initially intractable, otherwise resources are being wasted. If we know how a problem can be resolved, go ahead and do it!

Second, there is the 'ownership' of the project. The project has to be owned by its initiators to ensure the planning, implementation and outcomes of the project. The 'ownership' of the project will be shared three ways, the first two of which are essential:

- The person in the set, the set member, will have ownership in wanting to undertake the project to completion over a period of time. If the set member pursues a project without really wanting to do it then a lack of commitment to the project may mar its successful progress. The desire to undertake the project will be negotiated with –
- the second person, a 'client' elsewhere in the organization for whom resolution of the problem is also important. This person will act as the client who will negotiate with the set member to determine the purposes of the project, it's implementation and a review of its outcomes.
- The third interested person with some ownership in the project may be the person responsible for management development, the set member's line manager and/or our management developer in the organization who will wish to be assured that development of the individual happens in addition to completion of the project.

The set adviser and set may have an additional and useful contribution in providing a focus for the set member to determine the feasibility of the project within the set framework. The set member takes any problems in undertaking the project to the set in order that she can think them through with the support of the set and the set adviser.

Group project
This guide is primarily about projects and issues undertaken by individuals

which are progressed with a set. A variant is a group project where the members of the set are undertaking a group project on behalf of the organization. In this form the set divides the project work among members of the set. It is important to recognize and distinguish two features here which, if a facilitator is present, will need to be highlighted for the set. There will be team issues which the set members will wish to resolve and work with. There will also be individual issues which each set member may wish to bring to the set to reflect upon and progress. It is appropriate for the set to work on the latter. Where the issues are team ones it is better to go into team mode. For example, there may be conflicts in the group over the progress of work. The facilitator and members can aim to keep the distinction clear in order that the action learning set mode can be used for progressing individual parts of the project.

Personal development issues

At the other end of the continuum, the 'personal development issues' end, the set becomes the forum for staff to bring their issues to the set with the simple rule that the issue is one of significance to the set member. Sets are formed with staff who will potentially benefit from action learning and who voluntarily desire to become members of a set with other colleagues in the organization who do not have direct line relationships with one another. The sets commence, leaving the participants in the sets to address their own issues, problems and opportunities.[1] In this way participants start from where they are 'coming from' with their issues, problems and concerns. Examples could include:

● personal motivation towards work;

---

[1] We are sometimes asked why we use the terms 'issue, problem, opportunity' when inviting set members to bring what is pertinent and relevant to them to the set. We do this partly because we used to ask set members to bring a 'problem' to the set. The danger of using this term is that it might convey they may have a problem when they have not, that they may feel that they should have one and/or that they are a problem! There may indeed be a genuine problem eg a sticky relationship with a 'difficult' colleague. However, by using a wider range of terms we avoid centring on problems *per se*. Further, an opportunity might be, say, an advertisement in the press for a post to which the set member is considering applying but is uncertain because it is not in their immediate purview. This is not a problem – at least not at the outset. Similarly, a person may have a project they are pursuing which they bring to the set.

- line relationship as a manager with colleagues for whom the manager is responsible;
- completion of a research degree with field work in the manager's employing organization;
- prioritization of work for self and staff;
- future work direction.

As at the organizational end of the continuum, the set member could design some of the above issues and problems as a project with specific targets in respect of planning, implementation and review. Other problems may require more short-term attention and once they are resolved, the set can move on to other issues. For example, a set member may bring her desire to improve her working relationship with an 'awkward' colleague to the set, attention to which may mean the problem can be resolved fairly quickly. However, to the set member this relationship may be *the* intractable problem facing her at the time.

The choices along the continuum

Both ends of the continuum can be justified but do start from different perspectives. At the organization end is the view that any project initiated should have direct organizational benefits, with the manager as set member gaining her personal and management development benefits en route. At the personal development issues end is the view that the manager has her 'baggage' of skills, qualities, attributes and 'ways of seeing the world'. This is the starting point. Enable that person to work on her issues. In this way her management development will be engendered by those issues most significant to her.

In between the ends of the continuum are combinations of the above. For example, once the personal development issues have reached a degree of resolution, wider organizational issues and projects can be addressed in negotiation with clients elsewhere in the organization.

Both ends of the continuum have their dangers. At the personal development end, the manager and other set members may stay in a 'crisis-centred' mode, always returning to operational issues of concern. In the example above we gave the instance of a set member addressing the operational issue about working with an 'awkward' colleague. The set member could stay in the mode of always addressing issues like this one so that they recur again in one form or another. The set may, even with a set adviser, collude with this mode and the set member may not rise above the parapet to look at developmental issues.

At the organizational project end, the manager may tend to address the issues of the project, 'safely' ignoring her personal developmental issues by immersing in the content of the project.

Independent Action Learning Sets

'Independent' means that an organization is not involved in the creation of an action learning set or in determining the parameters of the set or providing direct resources for the set. Sets are formed by the members for their personal needs.

An independent set has advantages of being released from the constraints, demands and expectations of an organization. This freedom can be seen as positive in that there is usually an additional sense of commitment and responsibility to make the set happen, to meet, to continue and to ensure that the set works for each member. The negative side may be that the maintenance of the set imposes a responsibility in respect of time and resources that the set member may not be able to provide which the support of an organization can.

An independent set may also mean that a set member can bring issues to the set that they may not bring to an organizationally supported one, particularly where the organization requires a client-based project. Here another continuum can be introduced (see Figure 3.2)

In contrast to the organizationally sponsored set, the set member has complete choice and total responsibility for what she brings to the set. In Figure 3.2 by project/task we mean for example:

- producing a report or project to a deadline;
- how to work with a 'difficult' colleague;
- how to overcome being reactive in work.

Figure 3.2 *Independent sets continuum*

A reflective issue or problem brought to the set could include those examples given above in an organizationally sponsored set at the personal development end. We could add more here:

- what am I doing this work for anyway?
- what makes me do what I ought to do as opposed to what I want to do?
- how do I balance my work with the rest of my life?
- where am I going in my life?

A set member may well start at the task end but gradually (and even deriving from the task end) move to the more reflective/personal development end of the continuum.

Another advantage of independent action learning sets is that they enable those not attached to an organization to join a set. Here we include people who are home-based, those not in paid work and the self-employed who would like support from a set.

With an independent set each member can decide what to bring to the set without any accountability to external providers. The only accountability is to themselves supported by the other set members!

Sets created and supported by an organization need a champion in order to obtain agreement for this form of development as well as the resources of time allocation and funding of set advisers and possible cover of set members' work. Independent sets require to be their own champions in creating and maintaining the sets. This appears superficially a more daunting task.

Consideration of the need for a set adviser to facilitate an independent set may be an impediment on grounds of cost for the set adviser's time. However, as we will show in Chapters 6 and 7, depending on the skills that set members bring to the set, a facilitator may not be necessary. Alternatively, a set adviser could facilitate the set for a short period to enable take-off to self-facilitation.

This chapter has concentrated on the basic use of action learning sets in organizations and those independent of organizations. A feature of our book is the growing use of sets in higher education. There are particular characteristics which apply to using sets within the framework of courses that we consider in detail in Chapter 13. Otherwise, the current chapter can apply to higher education institutions as organizations in terms of using action learning for staff and management development purposes. Further, we have been members of independent sets whilst working in higher education.

Chapter 4

How a Set Works

This chapter describes the process of a typical set. Sets differ in the numbers of people involved, in the motivations of the individual members and the nature of the issues that they bring to the sets, but here we will describe the essential features of all sets and discuss the nature and rationale for divergence from this norm. The essence of the set is to create the atmosphere and use processes which stimulate learning from action. The actions take place outside the set meeting and often away from other set members. The set provides the focus for the reflective part of the cycle leading to learning from experience and the formation of plans for action informed by this learning.

What Does it Feel Like to Be in a Set Meeting?

Set meetings are made up of a collection of individual time slots. They can feel rather like watching television with a number of episodes from different series running one after the other. Each episode is more linked to the same programme last week than to the previous half-hour of viewing. It is like this in sets where each individual is working on their project (issue or problem) and what is happening in an individual's time slot is related to what they spent time on at the last set meeting but is unrelated to the topics that other people spend time on during the set meeting. The difference from watching television is that there is no passive observer role; every set member is active all the time. Apart from the facilitator there are two roles in the set: presenter and set member. These roles are described more fully in the following chapters.

Each set member brings their own project to the set. As described in Chapter 3, projects being worked on by set members vary from specific organizational innovations to very personal areas of development and from those which appear to have clear boundaries to messier and more complex issues. What it feels like to be in the set will depend to some extent on the type of projects and issues that set members are working on. Because projects differ, the atmosphere in the set is likely to change as different individuals take the presenter role. A manager working on specific plans where she has a free hand to plan changes and where the project is about making the best decisions on how to introduce the changes, will create a different atmosphere from a situation where the presenter is undertaking a more personal project to change their relationships with colleagues.

How it feels to be in the set will also depend a great deal on the personality of the set members and the degree to which the set becomes an arena for emotional openness. Sets vary and set meetings of a particular set also vary. Sets develop their own culture and degrees of openness and trust. It is important that feelings as well as thoughts are acknowledged as a natural aspect of reflection but how these feelings are displayed will vary with the climate and culture within which a set works.

Time

There are three ways that time impinges on the work of a set. First, there is the overall time cycle within which a set works. This is the length of time over which a set will meet and is negotiated at the outset. A usual cycle would be six months to a year with a review positioned after the first four meetings and at the end of the cycle. Second, there is the periodicity of the set meetings; how long betwen each set meeting. Again this is negotiated at the beginning, with set members agreeing the meeting dates some time in advance. Third, there is the time-keeping within the set meeting and the overall length of the meeting. As action learning sets have a clear structural arrangement the time-keeping in the set meeting is important for the success of the process.

The total time of the set at each meeting will require agreement by consensus, not majority. The set may agree to, say, three hours per session. The same agreement applies to the frequency of the meetings, for example, once per month. It is also useful to agree over what period the set will meet at the end of which a review of the progress of the set and set members will be held. This period will vary. We have tended to use between six months and a year.

The timing issue is one that the set may not be totally free to determine since there may be constraints for an organizationally sponsored set. The set may also be an integral part of a course and its life therefore determined by the course programme.

Time within the set meeting is generally allocated evenly to each member and it is important to make sure that time-keeping guarantees equity and effectiveness for all set members. If the set consider that one member has a particular need for more time at a set meeting, then with the agreement of the set the time can be reallocated. If, for example, towards the end of a presenter's time he is in the full flood of expressing a deep worry, it is sensible for this to be recognized, so that they can deal with it, rather than slavishly keeping to schedule. Time can be given away from one set member to another by negotiation and this is often useful when there is an issue that causes a strong emotional response in the presenter towards the end of their time. A set member's offer to give away time should not be accepted lightly by the other set members. It may be that a set member is unconsciously avoiding having the focus on them and yet may need the time and be sorry afterwards. The set member may misjudge his need for time, particularly in the early stages of set work. A presenter may feel that she has little to say precisely at a point when the set could be most useful, for example, when confusion makes the presenter unsure about her progress with her project or confused about the issues facing her. At these times challenge and probe from the other members can be very helpful.

If the negotiated timing is not adhered to, the set can easily become cosy and sloppy and therefore less effective. In order to enable useful reflection and learning for each set member at each set meeting, time must be a focus of attention. There is no coasting time at set meetings. When not presenting, set members are contracted to help another member in a support role. When the set meetings are being most effective and helpful they can also be quite exhausting events. For this reason it is important to have a comfortable and appropriate environment for set meetings. Set meetings are not cosy chats about how we are all getting on, they are working meetings with important outcomes for the future action of each set member. As well as leaving a set meeting having reflected and learnt from past action and set new action points, a set member is likely to feel stimulated by having contributed to this process for others.

How long should the set meeting be?

The time allocated and the numbers of individuals in sets is best decided on the basis of needs of the set members as well as practicality. Three hours is very tight for a set meeting with over five people. A good rule of thumb is that an allocation of half an hour per set member plus half an hour for opening and closing is a minimum below which the depth of set work would be seriously impaired. There is often the need for a break between individual set members' time to reorientate the mind and for physical comfort. A change of scene over lunch at least provides the opportunity to take a walk to refresh from the intensity of the set process as much as for physical comfort.

These timings look specific and inflexible and they have to be like this to some extent. Time-keeping is an important factor in the success of set meetings because the overrunning of one set member's time eats into another member's time. Sets which have unlimited time are very rare and so are sets that have too much time. Overrunning is a potential problem. This structure works but it is tighter than it looks. It is very difficult to stop an individual's time on the dot. It is useful for the facilitator or another set member to look after the time and to inform the presenter when she has about five minutes left. There is always more to say, more ideas to be had and rarely has everything been explored. But if the time is to be lengthened then some other individual will have their time cut. This is often managed in sets through another individual saying that they are willing to cut their time in order to carry on with the dicussion. This is a good approach although it puts at a disadvantage those who come later in the session. One way round this is to rotate the times that people have at different set meetings. This is a good idea from the point of view of different energy levels, the 'after lunch' slot often being the least favourite. It is important that time within set meetings is organized and changed by negotiation with set members.

09.15–09.30	Arrival and coffee
09.30–10.00	Round of how we are feeling
10.00–10.25	Presenter 1
10.25–10.50	Presenter 2
10.50–11.05	Coffee
11.05–11.30	Presenter 3
11.30–11.55	Presenter 4
11.55–12.00	Break
12.00–12.25	Presenter 5
12.25–12.45	Review

Figure 4.1 *An example from an organizationally based half-day, monthly set meeting with five set members from different departments*

09.00–09.15	Arrival and coffee
09.15–09.45	Warm up round
09.45–10.30	Presenter 1
10.30–11.15	Presenter 2
11.15–11.30	Coffee
11.30–12.15	Presenter 3
12.15–13.00	Presenter 4
13.00–14.00	Lunch
14.00–14.45	Presenter 5
14.45–15.30	Presenter 6
15.30–15.45	Tea
15.45–16.30	Presenter 7
16.30–17.00	Closure

Figure 4.2 *An example of a time schedule for a whole-day monthly set meeting with seven participants supporting a research degree*

The importance of planning

We have found that one of the difficulties in working in sets is finding a convenient time to meet. Set meetings cannot be squeezed into an odd hour here or there; they require more dedicated time and the right environment. Getting people together for this concentrated period of time requires planning. We have found that planning meetings for up to six months in advance is a good thing to do and at a minimum to plan far enough in advance to accommodate set members' normal planning cycles. Once in the diary a set meeting tends to be given priority above everything that is predictable. This is part of the commitment that members make when they join the set and can be written into the ground rules. Commitment and ground rules are discussed more fully later in this chapter.

Setting the Tone

Space and comfort – appropriate settings

Although it is probably true that a set meeting can take place almost anywhere, there are distinct advantages to taking care about the venue and its facilities. First, the set needs privacy and relative quiet for its meeting. It may be that sensitive issues will be discussed and possible that emotion will be displayed. It would be uncomfortable and restrictive if this were impossible because the venue was too public. Although we have found people's places of work good venues for set meetings (eg taking turns at each set member's work and taking the opportunity to be shown round the business at lunch time), it is important that the meeting room is appropriate and not an office where interruptions are likely. We have also found that people's homes can be a venue for set meetings – they often provide a degree of comfort and a relaxed atmosphere that is hard to find in a work context. The freedom to make tea and coffee or lunch as required and in private – and so continuing the set interaction uninterrupted – can also enhance the meeting. This venue may not be appropriate or possible where families would have their movements restricted and children demand the attention of their parent. Different sets will have their views of appropriate settings but it is important to consider the environment for the effectiveness of the set. In one of our course-based sets where the set was in a peer-assessing role for each other's projects, they requested the more formal atmosphere of the office for the set meeting rather than a living room. Classrooms were sometimes found to have inappropriate furniture for the length of meeting and to be difficult to book for this amount of time and size of group.

Freedom from interruptions

It is important that the set meeting be free from interruptions. Phones are the worst culprits and should be discouraged inside the meeting. We have found pagers and mobile phones equally irritating and use the ground rules to ban their use within set meetings. However, it is often necessary for people to be available for urgent calls or emergencies so one compromise is to allow time for phone calls to check on these at break times.

Comfort and energy levels within set meetings

To promote an atmosphere of concentration and reflection, nurturing and energizing must be important elements. Our experience is that the availability of tea, coffee, biscuits, etc can make a great impact on the success of a lengthy meeting. In set meetings, getting this right is important. Figures 4.3 and 4.4 describe ideas about how energy levels change over time and can be modified through attention to normal patterns of human interaction.

Communication between people in formal meetings can be greatly enhanced by the recognition that they are fundamentally the same as any meetings between people and can therefore gain much by the mirroring of normal human contact.

Everyday contacts between people have a pattern that establishes the beginning, middle and end of meetings. Aspects of this pattern can be easily transferred to more formal meetings, workshops and set meetings to enhance their effectiveness and make them more enjoyable for participants. A useful cycle to go through in any meetings is:

connecting – eg, hello, shaking hands, hugging, etc;
nurturing – eg, having coffee ready, asking 'how are you?';
energizing – eg, sharing latest events, short interesting game/joke;
working – eg, individual time slots;
rewarding – eg, thanking and offering outside set support;
leave taking – eg, checking on action points, next dates, goodbye.

These stages provide the programme with a feeling of wholeness and completeness which is missing from many group meetings but which can make a big difference to the effect of the meeting on the individuals. Working is the key reason for being in the group but working becomes more effective where it is built up to and reinforced as part of the total process of the meeting.

Figure 4.3 *Energizing meetings*

Beginnings

The beginning of a set meeting is important. We have found that setting the right tone at the beginning and finishing off the business well at the end are two of the main factors in having a fruitful set meeting.

Ground rules

In action learning sets we formalize the ground rules that all set members will agree to at the beginning of the process. These ground rules will then last for the duration of the set (six months or so). Most ground rules have confidentiality as their mainstay but there are many other rules that people may want to suggest. Each set generates their own ground rules specific to them and may want to review these after a period of time. A useful process for generating ground rules is brainstorming.

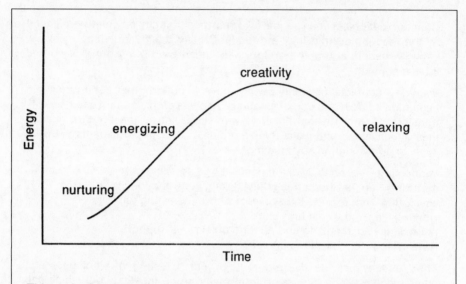

This cycle shows that energy-flows over time require periods of nurturing and relaxation. As well as the set meeting as a whole becoming more effective with the use of an approach to the event taking into account different stages within it, throughout the meeting energy will come and go. Keeping energy high for each individual may be greatly aided by periods of nurturing and relaxation. These periods do not have to be long to be effective but ignoring the need for them by rushing on to next business will make the meeting as a whole less successful. This cycle applies to the whole set meeting but also to the presenter during her time.

Figure 4.4 *The creative cycle, adapted from Randall and Southgate (1980)*

Brainstorming

Brainstorming is a technique for generating ideas quickly in a group. It has two distinct phases: the recording of all ideas on the topic or issue, and second the analysis and ordering/organization of the ideas. In the first phase the group appoints a note-taker and then everyone says whatever comes into their mind on the topic. It is important that the note-taker writes everything down as it is said even if it seems irrelevant. No one should comment on anyone else's thoughts but they can of course add thoughts of their own that were stimulated by earlier ideas. There is no turn-taking; everyone simply says what they think of at any time (so long as the note-taker can keep up) until all ideas are collected or nothing new appears to be being added to the list. It is

- One person speaks at a time
- Really listen to each other
- Don't make fun when I'm trying to be serious
- Aim to attend all meetings
- No smoking in meetings
- All set business is confidential to the set
- The ground rules can be changed through negotiation
- Don't phone at work about the project

Figure 4.5 *Example of a typical set of ground rules*

useful if the list is on a flip chart or white board so that it is visible to everyone the whole time. The second phase is the collation, analysis and organization of the material generated to make more sense of it. Here the group comments on the ideas and takes issue with them in order to find the final set of ideas, or clusters of ideas, to use for the purpose intended.

Ground rules must be agreed by consensus and the set members must feel comfortable to revisit them, to add to or change them as they wish as the meetings go on. They can provide a useful way to introduce a review of each meeting by asking the question, 'How well have we kept to our ground rules?'

Rounds as a way of starting a meeting

In other types of meeting we come in with our own agendas. We don't know anything much about the state of mind of the other people in the meeting and we often don't acknowledge them as people at all but simply as colleagues to be worked with for this particular time. We also know that the thoughts and feeling which a person has can be the biggest influence on how people are at this meeting. A set member with a preoccupation about something important unrelated to the project will make their contributions less effective in a set. This distraction is unhelpful. The set should, however, acknowledge the right of set members not to share their preoccupations.

In order to help each individual to feel closer and more able to reflect upon their state of mind and emotion we can do two things – (1) provide a forum for individuals to express their current state (often to acknowledge my preoccupation can release me from worrying about it for the duration of the meeting); (2) do something which links the individuals into the set: a set is more than a group of disparate individuals.

A round to begin

1. What's on top?

The simplest of rounds can be very effective. One we have used a great deal is just to ask everyone to spend a minute or two making a statement about what is on their mind – 'What's on top'. The other members simply listen and it is important not to comment or begin a conversation. It may be what is on top leads into what the individual wishes to bring to the set so comments should wait until later.

2. Trauma trivia and joy (this is described fully in Chapter 8)

These rounds should be voluntary in that a set member may say 'Pass' or leave a part incomplete. Rounds are most effective when they establish connections but do not run on too long. Allow between 10 and 20 minutes according to numbers and time constraints.

Negotiation of time within the set meeting

The main approach is to allocate time to individuals and to introductory and closing phases. Some sets like to take a more formal approach and prepare the agenda beforehand. One example is given in Figure 4.6. This proforma is used regularly by a number of sets which meet monthly as a way of helping to get into the meeting more quickly. Each member circulates their notes on the proforma to every set member before the set meeting. Time and ordering of the time is then negotiated very quickly at the beginning of the set.

My previous action points were:

What I have done since the last meeting

What I want to spend time on at this set meeting

Time I think I need

Figure 4.6 *Proforma for preparation of a set meeting*

The individual set member's time – the key to the process

What is an appropriate project to bring to a set?

By 'project' we mean anything that a set member works on in order to generate action points. A project does not have to yield anything in the form of tangible outcomes; the aim could be, for example, to raise confidence or to produce a major report. Some projects are problems – how to improve a working relationship that is difficult or how to bring a small business into profit in a declining market and so on. Anything can be worked on with the help of a set so long as the individual wants to progress with it. The will to act is often the first thing that a set can help the presenter to reveal. Action learning is about harnessing energy to develop both personally and as the result of our actions. It does not work magically; it requires from set members attention and effort. If a set member generates action points in a set meeting but never finds time to take the action, the result will be restricted to having reflected on the past. The most powerful action learning is making the link between past experience and future action. So it is best for set members to bring a project to the set that they really want to work on.

Another useful rule of thumb is that the project should not be trivial. If the set member could progress the project on her own, is clear about what to do next and has the will to do it then she has little need of the set to help her. A set can be most useful when the issue has been identified but the steps to progress are unclear, or when the presenter feels some discomfort with an aspect of life or work and is confused about exactly what the issue is. The presenter does not have to be precise about the project at the outset. Working with the set will help clarify thinking, sometimes in unexpected ways.

Although it is important to have a non-trivial project, it is also best not to work on too large a project. It is easy to take on too much and then become frustrated at the lack of progress. In thinking about the scope of the project, set members need to consider the time between set meetings and let that be a guide to the nature and scope of the project. Each set member needs to set action points that are possible to undertake in the time between set meetings. In set meetings presenters consider not just what the next step will be, but also the time period required for the actions to be undertaken. Where the actions take place beyond future set meetings, however, the set will be unable to generate reflection time. Wherever possible set members should choose a project that will be current for them over the anticipated life span of the set, although there need not be a one-to-one relationship between the span of the project and the length of the action learning set cycle. To some extent the nature of the project brought to the set will be related to the context of the set. If the set is formed to support a course, the projects will be related in some predetermined way to that course and similarly where a set is part of a working environment the nature of the project will relate crucially to that environment. These issues are discussed in Part III of the book. Some sets are formed without such clear contexts and in these sets the nature of projects can be widely spread.

Allocation of time to individuals

Allocation of time to individuals is an important feature of an action learning set. A set differs from a 'normal' meeting because there is not a free discussion of topics but rather an acknowledgement of the issue as tied to the individual whose issue it is. The issue remains the 'property' of the individual and the other set members' task is to support her in discovering appropriate actions in relation to the issue. In the set no one will take the problem away, rather they will support the individual who has the problem to work on ways to solve it or dissipate it. Set members will not resolve the problem; only help the presenter to decide what action to take (if any). The set members may challenge these action plans but they do so in order to help the presenter refine and specify the most useful action points. When the presenter is happy with her action plan the other set members can feel that they have done a good job in the set.

A set is not working as a set if individuals do not have their own time. But how they use this time can vary from person to person.

How can I use my individual time as presenter in a set meeting?

The usual approach to using set time is to report on the action taken as a result of the previous set meeting, so a useful format for a presenter would be to refer to the action points from the previous meeting and to reflect on:

- what I did
- what happened
- what was different from what I expected
  and/or:
- what I did not do – why – what I did instead
- what can I or have I learnt from this?

From this is generated a list of still-to-do action points carried forward, with set members questioning whether they are still appropriate or need refining, whether the time allocation is realistic, etc. The report can lead straight on to other action points that the individual thinks of – what I think I should do now – with set members asking questions like, 'What makes you think that is a good next step?', 'What would you expect to happen if you do that?', 'How will you go about that?', 'How long would that take you?', 'How important is that?', 'What do you expect to happen when you do that?' etc. Then the presenter can continue with:

- what is the issue now
- what actions could I take now
- what would be the best thing (specific) to take as action points.

This format is most useful when the individual is in the middle of a project which is going smoothly. The balance would be different in the first meeting of the set cycle when there were no previous action points or when the scope of the project is not fully explored. It would also be different at the end of the project when more time will be spent on exploring the future rather than in reviewing the past.

Types of process that sets can use

There may be occasions when a presenter wishes to use their time as presenter in a particular way in order to meet specific needs. As set members become more familiar with the action learning set they become more aware of how they can use their own time in the set most effectively.

A presenter can come prepared with a particular aspect of the project that he has identified as being a significant current issue and one that the set can really help with. The focus on a part of the project rather than all of it encourages deeper understanding from the set members and talking through in more detail with the set will help the presenter to open up ideas and see things from different perspectives.

A further strategy for using time is where the individual presents a problem to the set and then remains silent and asks the other set members to talk about the problem and to discuss ideas in relation to it for ten minutes. The presenter may learn more from this discussion while not being part of it as they do not steer the discussion. This may free up the discussion and open new avenues not thought of by the person whose problem it is. This phase must be very accurately timed with a cut off; it is followed by the individual asking for clarification or responding while the others remain silent, and generating action points as part of the response. This is a useful strategy when the presenter is lacking ideas on how to proceed.

There are varieties of this last approach, eg, the presenter talks about the problem with one other set member acting as an interviewer and the other set members play the role of observers each taking a different observer role –

looking at feelings, what is said, where there is a will to act, energy levels, body language, etc. There must be time for feedback with this strategy – its power is in the feedback given to the presenter which helps to uncover ways of thinking about the issues in a new way, eg, feedback like 'when you said that you frowned' can really reveal to the presenter an access to their feelings that they had otherwise denied.

Another variant of this is the reverse, when the presenter wants to talk through things and have the other set members say nothing at all. This is often useful when the individual is confused about the project or experiencing strong feelings about it. Just to talk can be valuable and help to open up the issues involved. A listening, attentive audience can be soothing and safe when things are tough. Often at the end of the time the presenter finds that action points are more obvious, or at this point the set members may be allowed to make suggestions for action points.

Sometimes a particular issue is so 'hot' that the set member can see nothing else and it is obvious that this must be the object of the presentation. At these times the atmosphere of the set can be emotionally charged. One of us facilitated a set where a member's line manager had put a block on the project and the time was naturally spent on the implications of this and what the member could do about it rather than on the next steps of the project itself. Similarly some crisis at home has sometimes meant that work on the project has come to a temporary halt. The set works on how to enable the set member to cope with the situation as it is rather than ignoring these important contexts. In these cases the set is dealing with exactly the issue that is stopping progress with the project although the ideas and discussion may not be about the project at all. Here it is possible to see the value of set work at its broadest – it is not just about progressing a project but about helping an individual to develop in relation to the project and to their life in general. Sets often become very close support teams for the individuals involved alongside project progression.

The process of set work is increasingly in the hands and control of the presenter who can, with some thought, construct their time to their best advantage. Different strategies will suit the presenter at different times and sets will discover their own patterns which work for them. Sets quickly have their own life and where one set will find multiple strategies are useful, other sets will be happier using a regular formula.

Ending

Action planning

The action plan is one of the main features of the set meeting and can be regarded as its main outcome. The aim is for each set member to leave the meeting with specific action points for their project that they have decided to do before the next set meeting.

The action points are the result of the time allocated to the set member and are decided upon on the basis of the discussion. They are, however, decided by the individual himself – they are not in any sense given to him by the set although they may have been taken on from suggestions made by other set members.

To be powerful, action points need to have certain features: First, they should be specific: Compare the following action points:

- I will talk to a few colleagues about the project.
- I will ask Jack and Mary to read and comment on my report suggesting a new marketing strategy and arrange a meeting to discuss it by the end of next week.

The second statement allows the results of the actions to be implied by the way they are described. It is easy to see what has been decided and therefore the results of the actions will be more easily seen. The advantage of specific action points is that they say how the action will be done rather than vaguely saying that something will be done. The formulation of action points allows the support members of the set to question the value of the action in relation to the issue. This questioning enables the presenter to draw up a list of actions that are clear and specific.

Second, action points need to be feasible in the time between set meetings. The most usual form of action points refer to actions that will be undertaken before the next set meeting. Thus progress on the project is kept up through a constant cycle of experience and reflection. If action points are taken which are unrealistic the effect of not doing them or doing only part of them will be demotivating. So one question for all set presenters is – although you think this is the best thing to do next, what is it that you can feasibly do in the time between this set meeting and the next one? What priority does it have and what competing things do you have to do? They are sobering questions – it is easy to become enthusiastic during a set meeting and to forget the restrictions of time and energy that affect us the rest of the time. We can't always get the balance right but one of the best ways of supporting a presenter is to look for the most effective action points in the time available rather than the ideal action points: What will make the most impact in the time available? What is the best thing to do first?

Two very effective time-management suggestions are the following (see for example, Bliss, 1976):

The Salami Technique which says that in order to complete something you have to take it in stages – to eat a salami sausage is daunting but to eat a few slices is appetizing.

The Pareto Principle (or 80–20 rule) says that it is 20 per cent of our effort that generates 80 per cent of the results. Thus it makes sense to think about what in the 20 per cent you normally do can be given more time and what of the 80 per cent you do can be given less time (Bliss, 1976).

Recording the actions

It is important that each presenter makes a note of their own action points and checks these with the set at the time so as to ensure that they are specific and understood. We have found it useful for a set member to make a note of all the action points and to circulate these under confidential cover fairly soon after the set meeting. This acts as a spur to action and is useful to feed into the next set meeting as part of each presenter's agenda. This simple rule encourages the set to focus on action rather than on discussion and the service to the set can be rotated among set members or taken on as a task by the set adviser.

Reviewing each meeting

Because action learning is essentially about reflection it is important to reflect regularly on the process itself. We normally spend a short time at the end of each set meeting making sure that action points have been adequately recorded and checking to see that each person feels that they have gained something from the day. Ideas on how to improve the process and ideas for other meetings are exchanged at this time and the allocation of roles for the next meeting is made – who will arrange the venue, who will send out the action points typed up, who will time-keep, etc. This review feeds in to the start of the next set meeting but it does not fully cover the whole process issues that may be there. For this reason a more thorough review is needed periodically. Reviewing is discussed fully in Part II.

The set progress

As the set becomes more established, members become more self-critical and critical of the process. New ways of running sets may be explored. The set members may feel more like taking risks and giving more explicit and directed feedback about interaction in the set. The exercise in Figure 4.7 has been used on courses where action learning is a basic process of learning and where the set has continued over an extended period of time or where set membership has changed at the end of one project before leading into a second project. The feedback is given in order to help all members understand how their work in a set is seen by other set members. It adds to an evaluation of the process and can lead to the establishment of new ground rules for the set.

Leaving and joining

When is a member of a set no longer a member? One person missing can alter the dynamic and because getting to know people is an inevitable part of set life, not getting to know some people because of their absence can provoke difficulties when that person returns. Keeping up to date with what is happening for people can enhance the effectiveness of the set and therefore not doing so can hold up the set progress for everyone and not just the individual who has not attended. To work well sets need commitment from their

---

Using the following list of statements, each set member takes it in turn to ask for feedback on one of the statements. This process of both asking for and giving feedback should be voluntary.

How do you find my set interactions in terms of statement number . . .

1. Helps me to find useful action points
2. Sometimes gets defensive
3. Talks too much
4. Listens attentively to what I say
5. Makes suggestions that are useful
6. Challenges me too much

A variant of this would be to base the exercise on a list brainstormed by the set members.

Figure 4.7 *Feedback exercise*

members. Set members often display a remarkable degree of care for each other beyond an interest in the project that individuals are working on. Rather like the best of colleagues, they want to help when times are rough and not just when things are running smoothly. When I feel that I have no time to spare for the set meeting can be exactly the time when the set could help me most.

Sets evolve in other ways – particularly in the ability of set members to take control of the process for themselves. The set advisers will model the facilitator process and develop the set so that the adviser becomes redundant to the process. Whether the set adviser remains part of the set beyond this time will depend on how far their own needs can be met in the set and how far the set feels that the adviser has become a set member. The ideal is for sets to learn how to listen actively, how to give support and challenge, how to receive ideas and how to ask for the type of help they need so that the facilitator is out of a job. This happens more or less quickly depending on the skill of the set and set facilitator and the attention given to reflection on the process through reviews. We have found that the set adviser quickly becomes part of the set and, as time goes on, less different from other set members. The facilitator leaving the set becomes more possible as time goes on, in that the set members can self-facilitate adequately. This can be an unpopular move, however, and may require some acknowledgement of a stage change in the life of the set, for example by setting aside time for review and celebration.

Closure

Even where the end point of a set cycle has not been predefined, at some time there will be a natural end for the set. Individuals have completed, with the set's help, the projects they brought. Becoming independent is an inevitable and natural result of set process. Actions produce results and take away the need for the set. Of course, often we have other projects that we could bring to a set, but the same group of people may not be the most appropriate for the new set.

It is important to acknowledge the end of a set and not let it drift into closure. Membership of the set has, most likely, been significant for the participants and they will have witnessed and shared their excitement, joy, laughter, anxiety, frustration and even tears. The life of the set is character-ized by stages similar to life in general: growing through tentative beginnings, through awareness and understanding, to maturity and eventual end. It is rare to find a working group that develops this closeness and it is therefore fitting to celebrate the process at its end: to mark the closure of the set as an event in itself.

New beginnings

Time and time again we have witnessed people who have been introduced to the experience of action learning in one setting, and gone on to join or set up new sets. The need for support is a natural part of life and the set experience is easily transferable to most contexts. Action learning sets have a very basic structure with some important key elements but beyond these it is a flexible and robust process. It is important to us in writing this book that without losing the simplicity and power of the action learning process we liberate it from becoming a preserved area for the very few. We hope that the description we have offered in this chapter will be seen as somewhere to start and that future users will experiment and extend the limits of the processes as we have done. This chapter has set the scene on how a set works. In the next chapter we discuss more fully the role of set members and how their interaction can foster effective action learning.

Chapter 5

Being a Set Member

The action learning set gives a particular structure to a group which, although very simple, radically alters the normal flow of conversation. The simple rule is 'one at a time'. Generally, time is shared within the set so that each participant is for a part of the time the 'focus' of attention. Their perspective and their issue is worked on by the whole group and in this time they control what happens. During this time as *presenter* the person presents his or her issue to the set in order to reflect on it and to design new ways of progressing with it. The outcome of this time is a set of 'action points' that the presenter decides to take on and which he or she intends to complete before the next set meeting. During this time the other set members act as *supporters*; listening, observing, commenting and questioning the presenter with the aim of helping in the exploration of the issue and in forming the new action points. The third role, that of *facilitator* is to enable this interaction to be most useful to the presenter. Because in 'normal' interaction in groups people rarely concentrate on one issue at a time and almost never work on one person's perspective on the issue at a time, controlling the process can require skill. As set working becomes familiar to set members so they take on the roles of supporter and presenter more easily and the role of the facilitator declines (see Chapter 6 for a fuller explanation of this role).

The aim of this chapter is to explore the roles of presenter and supporter and to make explicit what people do in these roles. The chapter will describe in some detail helpful aspects of communication within the roles and also things that are destructive to the process. In many ways being a helpful set member is the same as being a 'real friend' but more so. Friends listen actively and, through empathy with the individual and the context they are in, find ways of supporting them and enabling them to move forward. Friends also 'know' each other well and rarely pull their punches when important issues are at stake, whereas an acquaintance might collude with a pretence or 'front' put on to cover up important issues. The essence of an action learning set is to enable each set to learn from experience so that their actions can be effective.

What Do Set Members Do?

Action learning sets provide a safe, supporting and challenging environment characterized by trust and confidentiality where set members work on issues and solve problems through a process of reflection and action. The individuals in the set may or may not have personal investment in each other's projects but in either case it is not necessary to know details of the projects of other individuals. They contribute to the development of the other set members' projects only in so far as they help them to discover actions that they can take to progress the project. It is rarely necessary to know details in order to help someone to help themselves: listening can often be the key to helping another person solve a problem for themselves. As well as learning from their own projects, however, set members learn a great deal through their view of other set members' projects. Set members often have insights into their own projects while other presenters are having their time. There is also a more general development of understanding from the variety of projects and contexts that are brought to the set.

In action learning, set members aim to help each other to make progress with their projects but the members do not attempt to become directly involved with the projects of other members. (The only time this would not be true is where there is a set with a shared project. Here the time would be used to explore the individual's relationship with and progress on the project rather than a general discussion within the project team.) It is a key element in the success of the action learning set that ownership of the project, problem or issue remains with the individual who brings it to the set.

> I arrived with an issue I wanted help with. I expected help and to some degree I thought that help would be other people telling me how to do it but in fact what was much more useful was that I was helped to find my own solutions. The other set members didn't change my mind about what I intended to do so much as help me to see that my aims could be achieved more easily in quite a different way. (Set member at review)

One of the features of action learning sets is the 'one at a time' convention. It is not only that members attempt not to talk over each other but that they share time so that at any one time one member's issue is the focus of attention. Because each member is assured of this individual attention for their own issue at each set meeting an atmosphere is promoted where the giving and receiving of help is effective. The set members focus directly on the issue as it is perceived by the presenter and thus interaction is not a generalized discussion about 'the world' but focused on the person and their context. In the next section we consider the role of presenter and then move to describing the role of the other set members in the supporting role. Facilitation is the subject of Chapter 6. The skills introduced in this chapter are revisited in more depth in Chapters 9 and 10.

Presenting

The first question facing the presenter is always where to begin in describing the project to the set. The presenter knows she needs support and advice but how to involve the other set members in her issue and how to explain the context can be tricky. A good guide is to 'start from where you are'. Unlike most conversations, the set members can be relied on to listen while the presenter has false starts, repeats herself and presents disjointed and unformed ideas. They will not expect her to have the project in a nice neat package nor will they move on to another issue out of frustration or irritation with her inability to express herself clearly. On the contrary, they will see her stumbling words as an incentive to listen more closely, to mirror their observations and to reflect back what she has said in order to help her to get her story straight for her. They are indeed like the very best of friends who will not judge and will always give the benefit of the doubt that what is being disclosed is important and that they can help.

It is the *story* and not history that is important (Egan, 1973). The distinction is about the here and now as opposed to the past. I can describe the past as if it is remote from me and does not have any direct bearing on what I am doing now. Alternatively, I can describe the past as I view it from here – in this latter case the past becomes part of the story about what I feel now.

Feelings can be the best place to begin the story. It is in the here and now that new actions can be discovered and not in the past. It is what the presenter feels now that is the important information in this exploration the set will make. What is felt can provide a very rich source of questions for the supporters to ask and for the presenter to explore. Feelings express authenticity. The more that feelings are explored the easier it becomes to discover useful action points.

Where the project remains external and does not arouse any emotions it is unlikely to be a very important project to the presenter or to others. The nature of action learning is that it involves action; learning is not confined to the theoretical level: what I think may remain hidden inside me, but what I do is usually very visible. Where a project is seen as involving me as a totality rather than me only in my work role detached from the rest of myself and my life, then there is a real opportunity for personal growth and development through the project. The cycle of action and reflection becomes a personal exercise demanding more of me than the completion of a few objective tasks. Where I take on issues of real importance to me, action learning provides the encouragement to take real risks and to make real progress. Where I opt for an easier route, not allowing myself to face up to deeper issues involved in the project, action learning will help only with completion of the surface project. It is up to the presenter how deep they want to go. What is on offer is the chance to have the kind of support for change that is rarely available. It seems a shame to waste the opportunity on something trivial.

Learning to receive

Just as the main skill in being a support is to actively listen, there is an equivalent for the presenting set member in really listening to the questions that are asked and the ideas posed. It is easy to keep the blinkers of our own ideas and quite hard sometimes to accept that there may be other ways of doing things. The presenter has nothing to lose and everything to gain from having an open attitude to the responses and questions of the supporting set members. Really listening to their challenges and giving real consideration to their ideas can enhance the presenter's future actions greatly. If the presenter decides to reject their ideas then she will have done so from a point of full consideration and her own ideas will be strengthened by having considered alternatives. Learning to receive is also about receiving support. Learning to trust the support members to really want to help is often difficult when we are used to relying totally on our own resources and feeling that it is weakness to admit that we need support. Sets can be truly supportive only if allowed to be so. If the presenter allows herself to be vulnerable in a set meeting she will take great strength from the support of the set members. The great promise of action learning sets is their non-competitive spirit. Learning to rely on the

Time	The presenter's role	The support role
Beginning	Describing	Observing/listening
Middle	Exploring	Reflecting back
	Questioning Listening/thinking	Offering ideas (but not presciptions)
End	Exploring future actions Asking 'what if' questions Specifying action points	Questioning action

Figure 5.1 *Example of the progress through a presenter's time*

support of the set happens over time and is part of the establishment of the set culture. Set members do not deal with the issues and problems for the presenter, rather they enable the presenter to decide for herself the next actions to take in relation to her project. She does not go to the set to do the project, but rather to learn from the experience of doing it.

Asking for what you need

The set process is responsive to what the presenter needs according to their current state of mind and the type of project. At times the presenter might need to be supported and encouraged in order to progress. At other times the best support may be fairly tough challenges to the presenter's way of thinking, to help her re-evaluate her situation. Whatever the other set members think about what the presenter is doing, she remains the best judge of what progress means to her. By that same criterion, the presenter is responsible for helping the other set members to give her the kind of support she most needs. This means that the presenter can increase the empathic responses of the supporting set members by being explicit about the kind of support required. Asking for appropriate support becomes easier as the set gels and the process becomes more familiar. Presenters learn what kinds of support help them best at different times. For example, a presenter whose action points last time resulted in a crisis may feel vulnerable and want to be listened to with little challenge, while someone who is very sure about what they want to do next may want strong challenging questions in order to check out their ideas.

Taking control of the process

There are many appropriate and useful ways of spending one's time as a presenter other than strictly presenting. A presenter may ask for a brainstorming approach or he may ask to be a spectator while the other set members discuss his project. It remains the responsibility of the presenter to ask for the type of help they would find most useful.

The presenter must therefore make it clear when she is being helped and when the support offered is not helpful. If the presenter expresses herself clearly on this, the process will more likely develop towards a satisfactory conclusion: it would be useless to spend time discussing something that will not help her to generate her next action points even if the topic is generally interesting. For best results the presenter must keep the focus on her real issues. The other set members are trying to help and they can do so more easily if they get feedback on what is and isn't useful. Helpful statements like, 'What I really need is . . .', and 'That's interesting but I would rather move on to . . .', can cue the set members in to the real focus. Supporters would be within bounds, however, to occasionally question the presenter about changes in direction. Sometimes this may be an avoidance strategy and worth a challenge.

Action planning

In forming an action plan there are two distinct areas of concern. The first is whether the action is appropriate to the problem and the second is whether the action is possible in the time allocated. Perhaps the most important thing a presenter does is to generate action points to be worked on before the next set meeting. 'Good' action points have a number of important characteristics. They are:

- specific;
- clear;
- feasible;
- consist of the most important next steps.

Being specific and clear is easier after the issues have been fully explored and alternative actions discussed. The action points are likely to be more feasible if the context, including the constraints within which a presenter works, have been taken into account in their generation. The task of the presenter with the set's support is to try to meet these criteria as a result of their set time – it requires the full cooperation and energy of the whole set and it is the essence of good set work.

Sometimes the focus of the set develops and changes over time. One model would be the traditional project process: project definition, exploration, diagnosis, action, evaluation and review. At other times progress over time can move from one project to a redefinition of the project and to a refining of the focus for the project such that the initial description of the project is nothing like the description later on:

> I began work on a career plan for my future and moved through investigating my skills and past feelings about work. The project ended up being about me – about what I want from my life and how I want to spend time. It became much more personal than I had envisaged and I gained a great deal more from it than I had first anticipated.

> My project started with an aim to bring in a new computer system for management information; it grew into a reorganization of the management structure of the whole company.

Whatever the process over time the main criterion for success is that individual set members (and sometimes their line managers and companies) feel that progress and development is taking place.

Supporting

'Is what I am about to say helpful to the presenter?'

The best question that set members can ask in the support role is, 'Is what I am about to say going to be helpful?' This question will weed out those questions and comments which would only serve his own purpose – to give him information he wanted for himself or to make him look knowledgeable, etc. It is easy to underestimate the discipline involved in asking this question but the rewards for the presenter are enormous. To cultivate the attitude of real attention to being helpful is the key to effective set work.

Recognizing that each person is the world expert on their own problem

Only by believing that people can take responsibility for themselves can we really take part in action learning. If a set member describes his experience believing it is the same as that being described by the presenter, while the presenter is thinking that her experience is different, the advice will be useless, however powerful it was for the supporter's own situation. The important effects are when the responsibility for solving the problem starts and ends with the person whose problem it is. The task as support therefore changes from being how to help solve the problem to being how to help the presenter to solve her problem, requiring a different approach to support. Instead of suggesting the solution that would appeal to him, the supporter spends more effort helping the presenter to come to their own conclusions about what to do next. Advice is offered only rarely with the belief that what any set member would do is not necessarily what the presenter should do. When advice is offered it will be offered with a different spirit – 'What do you think would happen if you . . .', rather than 'I think you should . . .'.

'What does it feel like to be that person with that problem?'

In order to help most efficiently it is useful to cultivate an attitude which is curious and thoughtful about the way the presenter feels about the problem being discussed. It is usually the case that each person in the set would have a different reaction to the same situation so it is less than helpful for a set member to describe what he would do in that situation. It might be better to think himself 'into the shoes' of the presenter and think about how it feels for her. Some of this can be done through observation. If I look closely at how the presenter is responding to questions and listen carefully to the words they are using to describe the situation, I can often understand the emotional attachment that she invests in the project. Often a good question can start with 'How do you feel about. . .'. The answers are often surprising and revealing and can lead on to probing important issues in the situation that help in generating action points. This attitude is best described as empathy: the ability to share another person's feelings. Empathy is perhaps the most important attitude for set members to have as it provides the best data on how to help the other person. Remembering that I don't have to help solve the problem can be a liberation here. My responsibility as a set member is rather to help the presenter to help herself.

A spirit of trust and confidentiality

One of the first actions of a set is usually to set its own ground rules (see the example in Figure 4.5) and one of the most important ground rules is confidentiality. Sets work best in an atmosphere of trust where members feel able to disclose their feelings and thoughts to others without judgement and in confidence. Lack of trust can make the set impotent as individuals are unlikely to focus on real and important issues where they feel they will be ridiculed or that others will discuss their issue outside of the set. A ground rule of confidentiality can give a feeling of security and intimacy required for openness and frank discussion of difficulties and help to make action points make a real difference.

It is often said of learning in formal educational settings that 'you get out what you put in'. Similarly, in action learning the effects will become more important if you are prepared to work on an important issue.

There does seem to be a relationship between trust and personal risk-taking such that a person is more able to take risks with new ideas or new experiences when they feel supported. There is a relationship between risk-taking and development in that development requires us to stretch our abilities and skills to move into areas that are untried. One analogy would be learning to ride a bicycle. There is always a risk that the child will fall off, but with encouragement and support the balance will come. Balancing without the aid of a third wheel or a steadying hand requires courage and will to succeed. The parent cannot ride the bicycle for the child; he or she must learn the skill through practice and trial and error with help and guidance from an encouraging onlooker. So it is in the set that for the presenter to act to solve the problem or move forward their plans, they need encouragement and support to take the risks that are involved.

Listening

In most human interactions the convention is evenness. If I say 'Hello', I expect a similar reply. It is also characterized by turn-taking. I talk a bit about my idea and then I listen while you talk a bit about your idea. Occasionally this turn-taking is deliberately altered. For example, when I have had an interesting holiday, you may wish me to talk more than usual. At other times the discussion is not even because I talk too much and you 'can't get a word in edgeways'. In this latter case you are unlikely to find the 'conversation' rewarding. In discussions with larger groups the situation is compounded. Our interests are unlikely to be equally served by any one solution. We may have a clearly outlined topic for discussion but have very different orientations or objectives in relation to the discussion of the topic.

People have different styles of operating in a group discussion: some talk more than they listen, others like to observe the rest and think about the issues silently. All of us are capable of operating with different styles depending on our relationships with the other people, our interest in the topic under discussion, our anticipated beliefs about the results of the discussion and so on. The balance between how much we talk, observe, listen and think will depend on the mix of these various factors.

If I want to really support someone I need to know what kind of support they want; where they are with their thinking so far and what they feel about things. I can get this information mainly from two sources – listening to what they say and observing the way they say it and the non-verbal cues they give which reveal feelings and attitudes involved in what they are saying. Listening is a very important skill which we all have but in many situations we choose to use it only minimally. In communication with others our own agendas and our own thoughts often dominate while others are speaking and so we are not really attending to what they say. In the worst cases we are simply waiting for an opportunity to speak ourselves. Really listening means having the right purpose in listening (see attitudes, above) and it means much more than leaving silence for the other person to speak. This type of listening is often called 'active listening' because it requires a great deal of attention and effort that we do not normally associate with listening.

Much can be gleaned from observation as well as active listening. People often reveal their feelings in the way they look as they speak and in their body language. An observation like 'When you said that, you frowned', can generate feedback to the presenter that helps her to articulate her feelings and therefore helps her to uncover important aspects of the problem she is describing that can otherwise remain hidden.

Learning to give

A really effective set is one where members are willing to give support and challenge to each other. Learning how to give support and challenge is, however, not a trivial matter. We describe this here as 'giving' because the key is the spirit in which challenges are made and support offered. Useful challenges are made when the presenter is helped to think through her problem and come to a clearer understanding as a result. Useful support is where the presenter is enabled to move forward from where negative feelings were blocking her progress. The best help is when there is an appropriate match between the presenter's need and the type of support offered by other members of the set. In some ways support can be seen as the opposite of challenge, ie, when I am confident and clear about the issues, challenges can minimize the risk that I may be working with blinkers on. A challenge at a time of robust activity can be thought through and worked on without depression. If, however, a challenge is made when I am feeling insecure I am unlikely to rise to meet the challenge but rather to cave in under its extra strain. It is in times of insecurity and anxiety that I need support and gentle encouragement. People differ in their response to supporting and challenging statements or questions. It is important that set members and set advisers are sensitive to individual differences. What can be a useful perspective to one person can feel threatening to another. Set members attend closely to what the presenter wants from the set and do not attempt to give them what they believe to be 'good for them'. Although the set process is about learning, the set members do not take the role of teacher or parent or manager in relation to each other. Their role is accurately described as supporter where the initiative remains with the presenter and the set members contribute their support to this process. The skills involved in doing this are described more fully in Chapters 9 and 10.

Recognizing issues underlying the problem presented

One of the best ways in which the presenter can be enabled to progress with their project is when the problems being faced are explored in some depth. The presenter may be unable to articulate very clearly the problems and issues that are confronting her. If she is asked open and searching questions, however, she will gain insights that she could not generate on her own. For example, a problem that she first described might turn out not to be the real problem at all:

> I came with one project and ended up with a totally different project. The best thing was that the set helped me to realize that the project I first came with wasn't important at all. The real issue was buried underneath the project and once I looked, it became like the layers of an onion.

Thinking of the problem as an onion with layers on layers can be a useful analogy. A group of people working collectively can bring many different perspectives to help uncover the problem. A new angle can release a whole set of new possibilities.

Learning how to ask good questions

What is a good question? Answer: one that helps the presenter to learn more about her problem, herself or the context within which she is working. A good question is selfless – it is not asked in order to generate an interesting response or information for the questioner, rather it is asked as a way of opening up the presenter's view on their situation. There is a variety of good questions.

The open question – one which cannot be answered with a 'Yes' or a 'No', but requires explanation – open in that it opens up the area for discussion. Open questions are exploratory and ask the respondent to go deeper into her world in order to bring forth an adequate answer.

Reflecting back is a technique which is half-way between the noncommittal – 'Can you say more about that?', and the more formulated question asking for particular information. In this technique the listener interjects to recap some of what the presenter has just said. This can be by way of a summary or a mention of what the listener has taken to be the main points. This acts as a check to see if the listener has 'heard' correctly but it also acts as a check for the presenter who can think more about whether what she said was accurately conveying her meaning; saying what she meant to say. This type of interjection can be powerful in helping the presenter to share her issue with the other set members as it allows her to review her 'story' as she tells it. It is very useful towards the beginning of the presenter's time when the issue is being outlined and the listeners are trying to understand its implications.

Another good reason is one used often by a skilled interviewer – it requires a reiteration of the last few words of the previous response and asks for clarification of meaning. Thus, 'When you say . . . what exactly do you mean?'

A simple question that can bring forth many goodies is the question of the innocent three-year-old: 'But why?'. 'Why' questions, however, get answers that are rationalizations – 'Because . . .', and asking 'Why?' can seem like an interrogation. The presenter may not have an answer to the question 'Why' but will usually feel impelled to invent one. It is often better, therefore, to translate the 'Why' question into a 'What' or a 'How' which asks for an easier descriptive form of answer, eg, 'Why is that important?' becomes 'What was important about that?', asking for a description rather than an explanation. It follows that other powerful questions can also start with 'How', 'When', 'Where', etc – questions which require more clarification of the situation.

Good questions are rarely leading questions such as, 'If I was in that situation I would do XYZ – what do you think about that for your situation?'. This can however be appropriate towards the end of the presenter's time when she is searching for action points. It is easy for this to become a bit of advice in another guise and direct advice is seldom the best thing to offer, particularly in set time. Advice may be best offered after the set meeting rather than using time to describe your own situation in someone else's time.

Giving time for reflection

It is easy to fill time with speech, even if this is kept strictly to one at a time. This can work against the presenter who may have far too many thoughts to deal with at once. Leaving space for thought between questions and comments is a very useful strategy. This means that supporters must support each other by allowing the presenter adequate time to consider the comments of other supporters. This can be a frustrating experience. Most people have something they can offer and to remain silent while there is a burning issue to explore is not what we usually do. The presenter, however, may find silence the most liberating and useful part of the whole exercise. To be allowed, for example, to really consider carefully an observation made about my demonstration of anxiety can be the lever to my gaining control of a difficult problem. If another set member immediately offered another question the presenter might lose the thread of her thoughts completely and the impact of the observation would be lost. The inclusion of silence can mean that in a presenter's time some of the supporters may not speak at all. Counter-intuitive though this may seem, this might be the most helpful thing that they could do.

What room is there for manoeuvre here?

As in all problem-solving there are some solutions which feel impossible to take because they are too radical, the costs are too high or they are unethical, etc. Where any one person draws these lines will be an individual decision. Although it is important that a presenter is challenged about her chosen actions and radical suggestions are not outlawed, it is also important that a practical approach is taken to the future actions people take. Some problems can seem intractable and it is up to the set with its collective creativity to let the presenter find the 'eye of the needle'. When the presenter is feeling gloomy and despondent set members can help by being with her and keeping a positive approach. There is always *something* that can be done however small. What are the alternatives? What scope is there for change? If I can't do it alone, who can and who will help? Finding the scope within which a presenter has control, both contextual and in terms of personal willingness, is one useful focus for the set at such times. One warning, however: do recognize as real the difficulties that the presenter faces. The feelings of disempowerment are real to them. A good friend will help me to overcome negative feelings to feel refreshed, ready to tackle things. This does not happen through trying to pretend the difficulties are not there but rather through listening attentively and helping me to discover for myself that I can do something about it.

How to help someone to generate their own action plan

There can be as many good questions asked about suggested actions as there can be in exploring the problem. Don't let the chance slip by to question whether an action will be appropriate. Again the simple question, 'What do you *want* to do?', can be most powerful here. Another good question at this time is to ask, 'What do you expect to happen if you do that?' Other questions can be about the feasibility of the action – time available, the power and influence to perform it, etc. Another good question here is, 'What would happen if you did nothing?', and 'What would happen if this works to its most ideal?' Both these questions help in further defining the action points and assessing their feasibility. It is important that the set leaves sufficient time to concentrate on helping the presenter to specify action points before moving on to the next presenter's issue.

Preparing

As with most meetings action learning sets can begin more easily if everyone comes prepared. The simplest and quickest preparation is to read through the action points that were generated at the last set meeting. Each set member will have worked with his or her own, but to read through those of others will help to get thoughts in tune ready for the set. Set members remind themselves about other people and think through where they might have got to with their projects. This helps set members to be ready for each presenter's time. Some sets arrange to have more structured preparation, eg, phone calls in between the sets or sending round questions asking for a synopsis of the work done since the last set meeting. Suggested headings for such a form could be:

- Describe the main issues arising for you since last set meeting.
- What do you want to concentrate on in your presenting time?

- How much time would you like for this?
- What other issues would you like discussed?

The most important preparation, however, is for each set member to have completed the action points from the previous set meeting or, if not, to have thought through the reasons and to be clear about what they want to discuss at the set meeting. Nevertheless, at the beginning of the set meeting other issues may surface, to do with very recent events. This can make preparation redundant and it is usually more important to respond to these 'on top' issues than to stick to previous arrangements. For example, if one set member arrives in a state of notable elation (or depression) it may be inappropriate to wait until it is technically his turn and set members may agree to let him have his presenting time first. Alternatively, a set member may not be clear what they want to say; it is often the role of the set to help the presenter explore her issues or problems. Although one key to set working is the clear structure of the meeting, flexibility is a key concept in responding to the individual, the project and even the maturity of the set.

Another level of preparation for the presenter is to consider what type of help she would like from the set members in her own time. As set members become more experienced it is easier to think of the best way to use time as presenter. A presenter may want to use her time in different ways according to the type of issue she is bringing to the set and her stage of development in thinking about it. There is a continuum between one extreme where the presenter takes all the time talking, to the other where the presentation is very brief and the set members question, comment and make suggestions for most of the time. There are many varieties of process that are useful in the set (see examples in Chapter 4). Experimentation can help in finding which ones work best for each set. When set members think through the process that they want to use, prior to the set meeting, they are likely to greatly enhance learning in the time available.

Reviewing

Most set meetings will end with a brief review of the meeting. How do set members feel now? Has each presenter a record of their action points? Sometimes the review is more substantial, focusing on issues of evaluation of the process and interaction between set members. A good time to have a more substantial review would be after about five meetings. The more honest the feedback, the more likely that the set will develop into a positive experience for everyone. Feedback to the facilitator is also important. This will be a subject for further discussion in Chapter 6.

Chapter 6

Being a Facilitator

Sets can have a facilitator (sometimes referred to as a 'set adviser') or they can be self-facilitating. This chapter sets out the role of facilitators and examines how facilitators can contribute to making the set effective. We will examine what sets need to be effective without a facilitator in Chapter 7 on self-facilitated sets. To prevent unnecessary duplication, users of this guide are referred to Chapter 4 on the basic processes of how a set works and to Chapters 9 and 10 for personal and interpersonal skills used in a set.

Overview

The key purpose of the facilitator of an action learning set is to enable each set member to work on and with their own real issues. The facilitator encourages each set member to take responsibility for defining their issues, for action in overcoming a problem and pursuing an opportunity or task. This key role is also taken on by the other set members for each other as modelled by the facilitator.

For this main purpose to be fulfilled, an important subsidiary purpose is necessary. In addition to enabling set members to achieve their 'tasks' the facilitator has the initial responsibility of ensuring that the set works or functions as a set. Action learning sets are a form of group working. Maintaining the set as a group is crucial to enabling the main purpose. If the 'process', how the set works, is not attended to then the set will go into decline or destruct. However, in our experience the nature of action learning is one that promotes an effective group process.

The value of the facilitator to the set is underlined in another way. All set members take their issues, tasks and problems to the set. The facilitator does not take her issues to the set. She can therefore give undivided attention to the effective operation of the set and set members can, initially, give regard to their own and other set members' issues.

As set members become aware of the process that underlies action learning – how the set works – they begin to model the facilitator and integrate her facilitation and process skills into their own set practice. For example, the set members will soon begin to enhance their capacity to listen by implicitly recognizing how the facilitator attends to the presenter. Set members will come to action learning with personal, interpersonal and group process skills with varying levels of sophistication. The structured nature of action learning fosters the acquisition and enhancement of these skills.

Thus the facilitator's 'expertise' in facilitating the set is acquired by the set members. This transfer is important. The aim of the facilitator is her own redundancy! Action learning is about empowering people to take responsibility for action on the issues of their lives. For the facilitator to create a dependence in the set members is to limit the potential for that empowering; hence the placing of quotation marks round expertise. It is an expertise to be acquired and taken on, not to be subordinate to.

The facilitator plays a crucial role. She takes initial responsibility for the set working together through regard for the process. She ensures that each set member can pursue their issues. But what does this mean? How does the facilitator enable this to occur? There are two aspects to this process. The facilitator models how to *give* support and enables the set member to *receive* support from the other set members.

Getting the Set Going

Sets as a group

An action learning set is a type of group activity. Group working calls for good basic interpersonal skills which until recently have not been addressed in schools and post-school education. It has been suggested (Egan, 1976; Heron, 1989) that in British and American cultures we do not give much explicit attention to the development of our interpersonal skills. We would endorse that general view and discuss it in more detail in Chapter 9.

The way the group is organized is important. Groups can be classified in a number of ways. One is along a continuum from being unstructured to groups that are structured, the distinction based upon the rules or norms that are made explicit about how the group operates.

Unstructured   Structured
                                                                        Facilitated Sets
                                                                    Self-facilitated Sets

Figure 6.1 *Group organization*

Action learning sets fit on the continuum towards structured forms of groups. The structured nature of facilitated sets derives from the basic procedures adopted for action learning outlined in Chapter 4.

Life of the set

Like all groups, sets have a life that starts, matures and ends. Acknowledging sets as having a life helps us understand the set in terms of the feelings that set members and the facilitator can have toward the set. The facilitator's sensitivity toward that life of the set will enable the set members to deal and cope fruitfully with that life.

Facilitating a New Set

The facilitator at the introductory or first set meeting conveys the basic format of how sets work and how each set member can most appropriately give support to other set members and also best receive support during her time.

Rather than repeat them here we recommend that facilitators follow the guidelines set out in Chapter 4. It is important for the facilitator to keep the format details to a minimum to avoid giving the impression that the facilitator is going to be a talker or instructor. If brevity is paramount in order to get the set working (doing it is better than lengthy description) then we would simply emphasize the following points.

Most of the guidelines below are actually minimum ground rules for a set to operate. The ground rules can also be referred to as a contract. Additional ground rules will emerge which the set can agree. Whilst the guidelines are considered elsewhere (Chapters 4 and 5) they are included here for the facilitator to give primary attention to in the early stages of the set's life.

Warm up
At the initial meeting ask each set member to say who they are (if they do not know each other), what they do, together with a warm-up activity like:

- something no one here knows about me;
- trauma, trivia and joy (see Chapter 8);
- what is the best thing about my work or studies and what is the most difficult.

The effect is to ease any tensions that there will, quite naturally, be in the group. It is important that the facilitator engages in this activity, perhaps as a model by doing it first on this occasion. A warm-up activity is also useful to get the energy of the group moving (see Figure 4.4).

Confidentiality

The set members may or may not know each other prior to the creation of the set. It is critical that the set contracts to maintain confidentiality about other set members' contributions to the group. Material protected by confidentiality and not to be taken outside the set includes:

- what the other set members say about themselves, their content, how they may feel, what they may intend to do;
- how a set member operates in the set – whether it is positive, negative at times, or whatever.

It is perfectly legitimate for a set member to take their own content – how they felt, what they intend to do – outside the set. It may well be helpful and necessary for the set member to do so.

Conveying how the set is working outside the set may be appropriate, but with a caution. Set members tend to develop their own commitment to the set. How set members relate to the world outside the set requires some care. Those who are not members of a set, particularly in an organizational setting, could develop feelings of envy depending on how a set member projects the set. Mistrust or anxiety could be felt by those who are not members of a set. The set could be regarded as a type of 'in-crowd'. The formation of sets is an important consideration (see Chapter 2).

Timing and future meetings

The use of time is critical to effective set working. We examine the use of time in relation to the overall cycle of meetings, how frequently they meet, the length of time of each meeting and how time is used within the set in Chapter 4.

Making 'I' statements

When a set member takes her time and begins to relate her story (refer to Chapter 9, pp 141–2 for a useful distinction between 'story' and 'history') it is important to suggest that she (and all set members), when talking about herself, uses the word 'I' when describing something that she has been doing, how she felt and what she intends to do. This avoids the use of words like 'you' (meaning 'me' or 'I'); one (ditto), and people (ditto).

The benefit of using 'I' is that it becomes clearer that what the set member is saying is not only about her, but that she 'owns' what she is saying. Contrast the following where the set member is ostensibly talking about herself:

- 'If you get into our office late, you feel that you have let the others down.'
- 'If I get into the office late, I feel that I have let the others down.'

A simple change in words from 'you' to 'I', but we now know that she is talking about how she feels rather than pushing it 'out there' where she can avoid actually expressing her own feelings and create an ambiguity about whether she is talking about herself, the others in the office, or both.

Another common example is, 'It's not fair', when what we probably mean is, 'I feel unfairly treated because . . .'. It is important that as facilitator we model the owning of our statements.

The Relationship of the Facilitator to Set Members

The purpose of action learning is to enable the participants to take responsibility for their learning and actions and to develop and/or enhance their autonomy. Inevitably, in the early stages of a set the facilitator is going to take a significant role in guiding and directing how the set works. The aim of the facilitator is to move away from this dependent relationship to one where the set members achieve greater autonomy.

Heron's (1989) three modes of facilitation are useful to convey how the facilitator can move along a spectrum, as shown in Figure 6.2.

Hierarchical mode

Initially the facilitator is in *hierarchical* mode, directing the learning process, exercising power over it and doing things *for* the group. She leads the set for it is usually a new way of working with which the set members are unfamiliar. We are continually struck by how new a way of working it is to set members. This comes out at reviews when set members comment upon the effectiveness of the process and how unusual it has been up until that point to work in that way.

At this initial stage, adopting the hierarchical mode is entirely appropriate. To adopt another approach would be to abdicate the responsibility the facilitator has for the successful launch of the set. This mode of working means that the facilitator will clarify and interpret questions about procedures, the aims of set working, appropriate and inappropriate behaviours and interventions.

| Hierarchical | Cooperative | Autonomous |

Figure 6.2 *Mode of facilitation*

However she is also, even at this stage, modelling practice that will enable set members to take on a more participatory active role – ideally from the first set meeting. For example, she will encourage set members to support, clarify, question and challenge a set member. In this way participation is encouraged and set members learn not to let the facilitator alone interact with the set member whose time it is.

An important example is the tendency for a set member to give the facilitator eye contact to the exclusion of the other set members. The non-verbal and usually unwitting effect of this is to exclude the other set members from the dialogue and to focus the interaction on one set member and the facilitator. Whilst the facilitator may try to cast her eyes around the group during the interaction to non-verbally encourage the set member to include the set in his interaction, she may consider it more effective to be explicit and say that we do tend to fix eye contact on the facilitator because of their initial influential and hierarchical role. In this example we have the facilitator being in hierarchical mode about a process and behavioural issue – eye contact – designed to lead to a less hierarchical outcome – shared eye contact – from that point onwards.

Cooperative mode

As the set becomes more confident with the procedures, processes and norms of the set, our facilitator can move on to Heron's second mode – the *cooperative* mode. Here the facilitator shares her power over the learning process and different dynamics of the set *with* the set members and the latter become more self-directing in their interactions within the set.

Set members no longer require only the facilitator's interventions to prevent imbalancing or disorientating the process. The set is more like a rowing boat where the crew (set members) are integrated and maintaining the system of an effective set. If there is a tendency to go off course, a set member will intervene to make the 'correction'. The facilitator is becoming one of the crew.

For example, in a set one of us facilitated, the set had been in existence for six months when, at one meeting, a set member picked up a point made by the presenter and began a monologue about the need for the law to be changed in the area of the presenter's issue. This was picked up and pursued by another set member. A previously silent colleague intervened to say that we were in danger of getting into a discussion that would not be of use to the presenter, detracted from the presenter's immediate concerns and was also using up the presenter's time. This was a brilliant intervention made without disabling anyone in the set and without any intervention by the facilitator.

The facilitator may still act as a prompt and support the set when set members are not going to pick up something that is happening that is militating against the progress of a presenter or the set. For example, a presenter may be saying he wants to do something but is conveying non-verbally that there is no will apparent and the lack of will is not being noticed. Should the facilitator intervene? If other set members are not picking up the signals then it may be appropriate to intervene and ask the presenter what it is about undertaking an action that may inhibit or promote the action.

Autonomous mode

The next mode beyond the cooperative is the *autonomous* mode. Here the facilitator respects the total autonomy of the set members. They are now on their *own way*, using the set to meet their needs as defined by them. Our facilitator may still be with the set but she is giving more space to the set members to determine their direction. Here the main responsibility is to subtly create and support the conditions within which the set members can self-determine their own learning.

The fullest example of this is when the set becomes self-facilitating and our facilitator has withdrawn. We shall examine the working of self-facilitated sets in the next chapter.

Summary

These three modes deal, in Heron's words, with the 'politics of learning'. We adapt this term to mean the management of the set, who makes the decisions and how the decisions are made about what is learned and how learning takes place. We are also conscious that there will be swings back and forth along the continuum until the point where the set becomes totally autonomous. There may be external constraints. The set may be an integral part of an academic course which prevents the set moving beyond the hierarchical–cooperative modes. Similarly with a set in an organizational context, management may require facilitation to be a condition of the set's existence.

Core Qualities of the Facilitator

Given the above modes of relating to set members, what core qualities do we as facilitators bring to the set? The purpose of being in a set for the participant is, through the task, issue, problem or opportunity he is addressing, to release and enhance the set member's capacity for understanding and managing his life and development. The key question is, what climate can the facilitator model and encourage in the set that is conducive to that development?

The facilitator has to keep in balance the needs of the individual set member and the maintenance of the group. These needs can be addressed in two ways. First, what qualities does the skilled facilitator bring as a person to the set to encourage a developmental climate for set members? Second, how does the facilitator create a learning and developmental climate for the set as whole? The latter is the subject of the next section.

For the individual qualities we draw on Rogers (1979) who considered the core conditions for a climate of developmental growth. The first is that the facilitator is genuine, real and congruent. She is herself. As Rogers puts it:

> There is a close matching, or congruence between what is being experienced at the gut level, what is present in awareness, and what is expressed to the [set member].

In practical terms this means that when the set member is expressing a feeling or an attitude, the facilitator is aware of the feelings or attitude and in being genuine and congruent is in effect being with the set member. The facilitator is enabling the set member to be himself as he is. If the facilitator is saying in effect, here I am as I am, then this conveys that it is perfectly legitimate for the set member to *be* as he is.

The second condition for creating the appropriate climate for development and change is acceptance, or caring or prizing: Rogers' 'unconditional positive regard'. Rogers calls it a non-possessive caring. However, this unconditional caring is not a 'should'. It cannot be a contrived regard for then it would not be genuine. The condition provides a 'nurturant atmosphere not a forcing one' (Rogers, 1979).

The third facilitative condition is empathic understanding. This means that the facilitator senses accurately the feelings and meanings the set member is experiencing and she (the facilitator) communicates this understanding to the set member. The purpose of empathizing is to understand where the set member is coming from and is. This enables the set member through his response to gain a clearer understanding of his world and behaviour. The empathy enables the set member therefore to have more control over his world. We consider empathy in more detail in Chapter 10.

Given the above conditions, an important proviso needs to be made. The facilitator and the set are not working in a social vacuum. We all bring our values to the set and it is important for the set to consider the processes by which they wish to work, like the relationship between facilitator and set members. In addition, facilitators and set members are increasingly concerned with challenging the many ways in which complex patterns of domination and inequality are maintained. An example can be drawn from Weil and McGill (1990):

> The onus for raising . . . issues is also often put upon those who have most to lose. For example, in largely male or white groups, it is common for members of oppressed groups to be seen as 'the problem', or as 'having a problem' that is not 'the group's' concern. Equally, when women or black people try to highlight aspects of their own experience, which may differ from that of others in the group, they can be seen as disrupting the status quo.

Therefore, if a set member or the facilitator feels that an assumption is being made about them which needs to be challenged, the conditions exist explicitly in the set for the challenge to be made without the challenger being made to feel outside the norm. We refer to this in greater detail in Chapter 14 under the sub-heading 'Personal and relationships development and empowerment.

Creating a Learning Climate

What climate is our facilitator endeavouring to create in the set? By 'climate' we mean the most effective conditions for learning by set members. Such a climate enables:

- each set member to achieve whatever tasks they bring to the set – the set makes a difference;
- set members to acquire and enhance their personal, interpersonal and group facilitation skills;
- the set becoming collectively an effective learning community;
- (optional) the set becoming an effective self-facilitating set.

For the organization sponsoring action learning we could add:

- benefits to the organization in enabling individuals through the use of sets to foster change and organizational learning.

We have discussed the other specific contributions facilitators can make to encourage effective set working. We have also indicated how set members can contribute to the quality of the set (Chapter 5).

What does the climate look, sound and feel like to the set? Climate is, we hope, a helpful word but we could also use the word 'culture'. In defining culture, McLean and Marshall (1988) admit that:

> It is not easy to define culture . . . we are familiar with it, know of its existence, recognise aspects when they are pointed out and yet find it very difficult to say very clearly what it is.

However, they draw on management writers who have attempted to define it in organizational contexts. Here are a few:

> . . . how things are done around here (Ouchi and Johnson, 1978).
> . . . the taken for granted and shared meanings that people assign to their social surroundings (Wilkins, 1983).
> . . . the collection of traditions, values, policies, beliefs and attitudes that constitute a pervasive context for everything we do and think in an organisation (McLean and Marshall, 1983).

Most of our experience of sets has been in organizational contexts, in which the set members bring with them their own backgrounds, together with the way in 'which things get done around here' including their perceptions of the history of the organization, its primary tasks, size, where it is geographically and its current senior management which reflects aspects of the power base.

Action learning set culture

Set members are part of the culture they work in and they bring that with them to the set. The set, however, even if created with the agreement of an external (to the set) senior manager has the opportunity to create its own culture. This cultural opportunity could be said to be a sub-set of the culture of the main organization or it could differ from the main organizational culture. Indeed it could be argued that if a newly created set were simply to replicate the culture of the organization, what would be the point of creating it in the first place?

Thus we have a cultural justification for the creation of action learning sets. If sets are about the development of individuals in an organization, then sets should have a climate or culture conducive to set members' development. This is a good reason for using sets in organizations in order that employees do not get stuck in 'the social glue that holds the organisation together' (Baker, 1980, in McLean and Marshall, 1988) where the social glue paralyses individual and managerial development. Any organization which adopts action learning is at least espousing that it wants to support development of individuals, organizational learning and change.

This cultural justification for creating sets based in organizations leads us to the culture or climate that can be created for action learning sets.

The conditions for the learning culture
Clearly, the intention should be to create a learning and developmental culture. This is obvious when stated, but what are the characteristics of a learning and developmental culture in the organization that is a set? Here we draw upon and adapt Hawkins and Shohet (1989). For us a learning and developmental climate or culture is one that:

- Emphasizes the potential that all different work situations have for learning, both individually and collectively. A set's work can take any learning opportunity that is relevant to the set member and create the conditions for learning.
- Problems and crises are seen as important opportunities for learning and development. Major crises are seen as growth points, and the culture of the set is one where it is safe to take risks. Failure is seen as an event to be learnt from, rather than to be depowered by. An example is of a set of colleagues working for the same organization, one of whom was under threat from a resident on an estate. The set member felt frightened and immobilized by the situation. This was shared by colleagues in the set who could empathize readily in the same role. The set could have become immobolized by the feelings expressed. However, the expressed feelings gave energy to the set members that enabled them to move on to reflect about the context of security in relation to the new roles that they had with the organization.

Learning came through that shared concern, a realization of effective but simple security needs.

- Good practice emerges not from reaction to crises but from set members balancing all parts of an activity, from action, to reflection, to new thinking, to planning and then back to action. This is what happened in the example above. There was not simply a reaction to a very real crisis. The set member whose problem it was initially moved from an emotional reaction to the event, through her meanings of the event in collaboration with other set members, toward new meanings and actions. It was a process involving set member feelings, reflections on concrete experience, new and challenging thinking, shared planning, a range of options and subsequent actions.
- Individual set members take time out to reflect on their effectiveness, learning and development. This becomes a cooperative process rather than an individual one or one that happens rarely for the individual.
- The set encourages feedback both from other set members and back in the daily workplace.
- The set encourages emulation of good set practice elsewhere in the organization so that a learning environment is transferred.
- Time and attention is given to individuals. The starting point is where they are coming from, recognizing their individual needs.
- Learning and development are seen in the set as active concerns which results in action and further learning.

The conditions set out above for a learning culture in action learning are the espoused conditions. We can say that these are the conditions that should prevail. Whether they do or not will be up to the facilitator in the first instance, and as the set gathers experience the whole set will embrace it by putting the above desirable conditions into action. It is the difference between *saying* what should happen and actually *doing* it (Argyris and Schon, 1978).

Reflection and Review

Reflection and review can take a number of forms:

- reflection, evaluation and feedback at the end of a presenter's time;
- review of a set meeting at the end of the meeting;

- review of the set after a period and series of meetings
  - about the set process
  - about the norms of the set;
- review of the achievements of individuals in respect of
  - achievement of the tasks undertaken during the period
  - learning about self, the set process and relationship to others outside the set.

Reflection, evaluation and feedback at the end of a presenter's time

At the end of the presenter's time a brief opportunity can be taken for the presenter to reflect with the set upon the process by which he came to his actions. He may give feedback about which questions, facilitations and interventions he found helpful and less helpful. He may also ask for feedback about how he reflected upon his issue – the content. The reflection about process is the means by which the set learns about set (and group) working.

In this way the set and its members build up their learning from experience – they learn how to use their learning to each person's and to the set's advantage. At the same time they are creating the climate for learning.

Set meeting review

Set meetings usually concentrate on each set member and the time allocated to each. In the early stages of a set's life it may be appropriate to spend 10–15 minutes near the end of the set meeting reviewing how the set has been for set members. A set review can include the following headings for consideration:

- One thing that I have gained from being in the set today.
- One thing I have gained/learned about the way the set works.
- Something I would like the set to consider that I am not yet sure about.
- Something I want to share that I have difficulty with when I am presenting and/or when I am a set member giving support to another.
- Something I want to say about the set, myself, the set adviser, another set member.

These headings are a suggested range from which a facilitator and set members can select or indeed add to. They are not intended for use all at once and certainly would be overwhelming and not containable in the time allocated above.

The feedback (see Chapter 10 on giving and receiving feedback) to the set will provide positive impressions of what is being gained and learned by set members. It will also provide the set and the facilitator with an indication of the impact that the set is having upon set members. For example in one set the most significant impression for one set member was that:

> For the first time in a group I have actually been listened to and heard without anyone interrupting and contradicting me.

In the early life of the set it is better to engage in the doing of action learning than to discuss what action learning is supposed to be about. There is a tendency in our culture to go into discussion and abstraction about an activity rather than just doing it. The doing of action learning will very soon provide a huge resource from which to review and reflect. Let the practice and doing emerge before reflection; otherwise there is little 'material' on which to reflect!

Periodic review

When this takes place is up to the set unless there is an organizational requirement for an 'in-house' review. To let the set get into the flow of action learning is very important. If the set has agreed to run for one year with 10–12 meetings we would suggest a review at the end of six months and at the end of the year's cycle. The six month review could use the time allocated to the set meeting or allow one or two hours after the set meeting.

Figure 6.3 shows a typical review used by us for set members belonging to one organization. The action learning set was an acknowledged and integrated part of their management development.

We will take the numbered questions in Figure 6.3 to identify the reasons for each set of questions.

Question 1 gives the set member the opportunity to reflect upon the impact of the set from the standpoint of the set member personally, in relation to her personal working practice and interpersonal relations. Typical responses under this heading have been the following:

> I have found a place that I can unload my burdens.
> I feel that I matter.
> I now plan my work in a much more effective way.
> I am now more confident in managing my staff and have learned how to challenge staff who were previously not pulling their weight.

Question 2 is about making the processes inherent in action learning sets explicit. Processes refer to *how* the set works to enable the set to be effective for each set member. This aspect of the review is very important. Set working

1) What have I gained/learned from the set or done differently as a result of the set:
   - for myself
   - for my work in relation to:
     - my personal work practice
     - my colleagues and staff?
2) What have I gained/learned in terms of my understanding of the *process* of the set that I have applied in my work?
3) What have we gained as a group?
4) How can I/we improve the operation of the set to make it more effective?
5) How do I wish to utilize the set in the next year?
   and/or
   Where do I go from here?
   and/or
   What issues do I wish to bring to the set that are important to me and my work?
6) How may we link up, and to what purpose, with the other staff in the department who have experienced/are experiencing action learning?
7) Are there any implications for the department as a result of the operation of the set/s?
8) Any other issues you may wish to raise.

Figure 6.3 *Action learning set review*

employs interpersonal skills (see Chapters 9 and 10) that are central to being an effective manager. For example, a manager has a basic requirement to be able to listen to colleagues and staff who are responsible to her. Simple enough. But we rarely get the opportunity to get feedback and to reflect on our capacity to listen effectively. The process of action learning provides a kind of living laboratory to get that feedback, reflection and practice. For many of our sets, participants have remarked along the following lines about this:

> I never realized how important it was just to listen.
> I now give my staff the time to really listen to them.

When we asked Question 2 initially we found that some set members were a little nonplussed by it. We realized that there was a more basic lack of clarity on the distinction between task and process. The distinction between task – the content of what was under consideration, eg, a set member's project, task or problem – and process – *how* the set worked to enable a set member to address their project – was quite new to some set members. This led us to provide supplementary material to support and prompt their reflection on this question with a statement of the basic skills they employ in the set that are part of the process. This is set out in Figure 6.4.

Figure 6.4 poses questions about the skills used in sets, the opportunity to reflect upon how the individual set member works in the set, what may be transferable to other situations and what values are identifiable that could be emulated elsewhere.

Question 3 moves from the individual to the group. Whilst this is a personal reflection on the set member's view, it can be incorporated in a collective reflection at the review meeting. Examples include:

Trust occurred amongst the group. This helped me and others open up and deal with things I felt vulnerable about

As a group we have become more powerful. Powerful in the sense that we are

---

There are a number of basic (but sophisticated) skills that we bring to all interpersonal situations. An action learning set places significant emphasis on some of these. Examples include our skills of:

- listening
- questioning
- giving and receiving feedback
- appropriate disclosure
- empathy
- challenge and confronting
- observation and feedback
- reflection
  - of my practice – on what I bring to the set
  - of the process of the set – the way the set works
- time management
  - my own time
  - managing the time of the set
- personal planning

How has your use of these skills changed/enhanced as a result of the set process?

Another key to the review/reflection of the set is identifying the values that underpin effective working of the set which you may wish to identify. How might you carry those values (if you wished to) to other areas of your work?

Figure 6.4 *Action learning set reviews: process skills and reflection* better equipped to provide solutions to problems rather than just moaning. It has also been useful for individuals to tackle problems after sharing them in the group. (This was a set where the set members all had the same job, but worked separately.)

Question 4 is designed to bring out set members' ideas on how they think the set could be improved. It places them in constructive critical mode. The question is designed to elicit positive suggestions rather than whinges. Question 5 invites a set member to ask how she wishes to use the set in the period following the review.

Question 6 is appropriate to organizations using action learning sets as a vehicle for management development where sets have been created. The question is designed to supplement any intentions senior management or those responsible for the creation of sets may have. Question 7 is linked. Action learning may have implications for the organization in terms of its capacity to collectively learn and therefore to transform itself.

Question 8 is a self-explanatory sweep-up question for set members.

The review process can be undertaken by the set members and the facilitator alone. However, in an organizational setting where set members are sponsored by their line managers, it may be appropriate to have the review with the line manager(s). In the above example the review took the following stages:

- agreement by the set members and facilitator (one of us in our capacity as consultant facilitator to the organization) to undertake the review and to invite the chief executive to the review;
- agreement of the chief executive to take part in the review. It was agreed that the feedback would be provided at the commencement of the programme of action learning for this group of managers;
- two page review designed by the facilitator (Figure 6.4 in an A4 format with spaces for completion of responses) given to all set members at least one week prior to the meeting with the chief executive;
- the review meeting takes place using the responses as an *aide-mémoire* for the set members;
- review meeting led by the set members presenting their analysis to the chief executive as a lead-in to a dialogue about the effect of the set on them and their work;
- facilitator at the review meeting to listen to the presentation and dialogue with occasional contributions;

- agreement of outcomes and negotiation of next stage of the life of the set – to continue for a further year with the facilitator, to have a further review with the intention of becoming a self-facilitating set beyond that point.

Reviewing the norms of the set

At the commencement of the set the facilitator guides the set and establishes, with set members, the basic ground rules upon which the set will be organized and run (see Chapter 4). Setting the ground rules means that the set has created explicit ways about how it wishes to work. For example, a basic ground rule will be that one person speaks at a time. Simple, yet crucial for effective set working.

As the set progresses over a few meetings, other ways of working begin to emerge that may be obvious to everybody and articulated, for example, 'Have you noticed that we are tending to slip over the time allocated for each set member with the effect of diminishing the time available for whoever takes the last slot?'. This can then be considered and the tendency modified.

However, not all ways of working are articulated or apparent to the set. The facilitator has a responsibility, because of her greater experience, to focus on what is happening that is not being said, but she may also not be conscious of all that is happening.

Examples of ways or patterns of working that can emerge without the set consciously realizing it include:

- one set member tends to ask fewer questions of a presenter than the others;
- a set member tends to come in first and quickly after the presenter has made his initial commentary;
- the facilitator gets into 'rescuing' a particular set member when the latter is struggling to find her own solution;
- a set member regularly avoids making specific the actions that he will take on between set meetings and talks generalities instead.

What is happening within the set, which these examples convey, is that the set is not noticing that some patterns of working are emerging that may implicitly limit the effectiveness of the set or the work of a set member.

Sets can, like any group, begin to unconsciously develop unstated patterns or norms, some of which can limit the effectiveness of the set. The set can begin to collude and become not just a safe place, but too safe a place. The set may get into a position where it never challenges a set member who is perhaps unconsciously seeking collusion in his way of seeing the world.

1) The unwritten rules of this set are . . .
2) What I find it hard to talk about in this set is . . .
3) What I think we avoid talking about in the set is . . .
4) The hidden agendas that this set carries are . . .

Figure 6.5 *Exploring the norms and dynamics of the group*

These patterns or norms of behaviour need not be limiting. For example a norm may emerge that set members start to bring a 'present' to the set, like biscuits. Such norms can 'oil' the set and help to make the interactions more effective and relaxed.

How can the set uncover these implicit norms and review them to assess their value to the set? The set can agree to put aside time in a meeting or outside to consider the norms and dynamics of the group. Figure 6.5 provides a few open-ended questions for set members (and the facilitator) to consider individually and then to discuss in the set, an activity adapted from Hawkins and Shohet (1989).

This activity is one where safety and trust need to be present.

A way of helping to foster an additional sense of safety may be to carry out the following activity first.

Hand three small cards times the number of set members plus facilitator to each person and ask them to record on each of the three cards one positive thing – a word or short phrase – about each person in the set. (If there are five set members plus the facilitator, each person should have 15 cards with one attribute per card.) On the other side of each card print the name of the person the attribute applies to. The cards are not signed by the author. The cards are placed in the centre, name side up and shuffled. Each person in the set is then given their cards name side up.
Each person may say how they feel if they wish to – but not to ask who wrote what!

Figure 6.6 *Positive feedback activity*

Review of individual set members' achievements

Here we are referring to additional reflection and review where the set member has completed a project for a client in the set member's organization and/or a project that has been completed as part of a course leading to a qualification. The project may have been documented. However, it is valuable to ask a set member to compile a reflective document which highlights what she has learned from undertaking the project and what she has learned about learning in the process (see Chapter 12 on levels of learning).

Chapter 7

Self-facilitated Sets

This chapter is intended for those practitioners of action learning who wish to participate in self-facilitated action learning sets, that is, sets operating without using a facilitator (set adviser). We will explore what we consider to be the attributes and particular needs of self-facilitated sets.

In Chapter 3 we describe the contexts in which self-facilitated sets can be used. We would recommend that readers also refer to particular chapters that are also relevant to the operation of self-facilitated sets. Chapter 4 outlines the set process, the basic insights, procedures and processes by which a set works; Chapter 5 conveys the essential roles of set members as presenters and enablers of the presenter; Chapter 6 deals with the role of the facilitator and gives the self-facilitated set member an insight into the skills and attributes necessary for each set member to take on; Chapters 9 and 10 underpin the skills required for effective set interaction by addressing skills development. Potential self-facilitated set members who have few facilitation skills are recommended to use the chapters mentioned above.

We use the term 'self-facilitated action learning sets'. Some writers and practitioners have referred to self-development groups (Pedler *et al*, 1991). We would distinguish a self-facilitated set from a self-development group by the former using explicit action learning processes.

We also make a distinction between self-facilitation and unfacilitated sets. It is a small but important point. Self-facilitation means that all set members consciously take on the role of facilitation in order to progress the set meeting. Each set member takes and shares responsibility for facilitation as part of their set membership. Only when being presenter will they relinquish that responsibility.

Benefits of Self-facilitated Sets

When we started our own self-facilitated sets we used the action learning approach because it gave a coherent structure and way of working that combined individual action and reflection as well as an effective means of maintaining the group. Often, when people get together for a purpose in groups, the result can be failure or group destruct because little attention may have been given to how the group will work and maintain itself. The action learning process has a balancing and sensitive format which meets the needs of members and the group as a whole. The action learning way of working in groups does not guarantee success, but it does reduce the chances of failure. Action learning methods are also very explicit and clear. This makes it easier for learners new to group working to practise, reflect and add to their repertoire of skills.

Effective use of private and public sector resources

We believe that organizations will need to use self-facilitated groups more frequently as they move from hierarchical and rigid forms of working to flatter, more flexible structures and more fluid forms of working.

Developmental activities for staff can be resource-hungry and wasteful if the activity does not lead to pay-offs for the organization and the individuals experiencing the development. Later in this chapter we show how an organization can use self-facilitated sets to promote staff and management development even though an external facilitator may be used to initiate the process. In Chapters 11 and 12 we consider how sets, whether facilitated or self-facilitated can contribute to the learning process for the organization.

Structured group learning in higher education

Throughout the UK and in the industrialized nations there is a trend to mass higher education. This is happening without a commensurate matching of staffing. Basically, teaching staff face higher numbers of students from a greater diversity of backgrounds. The one-to-one or one-to-few tutorial or seminar is going to be less common. Learners are going to rely much more on their own resources of time and application than in the past. Learning how to learn will be the premium challenge for the learner and their teachers. For learners to become flexible and self-managed will require methods which enable that to happen. Self-facilitated action learning offers one path through higher education expansion which can ensure that the experience of learning is a positive one where real learning is enhanced rather than being diluted by numbers. Teachers can use action learning methods to enable that positive experience to happen. Facilitated sets can be used as a means of transition to self-facilitated sets. We explore the potential in greater detail in Chapter 13.

The Brighton Experience

Our initial experience of action learning was through participation in self-facilitated sets. We were members of self-facilitated sets before becoming set advisers in companies, higher education and the public sector. In the description below we will draw upon that experience, with additional reference to McGill *et al* (1990).

Our interest in this form of action learning derived from our work in higher education on experiential learning and our desire for student learners to have much greater autonomy in their learning. Action learning provided a promising vehicle for postgraduate courses in management for part-time students.

As part of the process of building up an experienced team for the postgraduate management development courses and in the spirit of learning from doing, an interested group of staff began meeting as an action learning set with one of us as a member of that initial set. However, it rapidly became clear that action learning could be used much more widely than this. It offered staff as well as students a means of addressing and learning from their own concerns and problems.

At its formation the set comprised five persons: four with academic and one with administrative responsibilities; three men and two women; ages ranging from 32 to 47; white and able-bodied. The only common denominator deliberately built in at the beginning was that each person had a specific responsibility which placed additional work demands on them and their relationship to the institution and their colleagues. It was from these 'additional demands' that most set members drew their initial problem statements for the tasks they wished to work on with the set. We refer to the experience in 'The initial Brighton self-facilitated set', below.

From the outset there were three important ways in which this set differed from the traditional notion of an action learning set. First, action learning sets in organizations tend to have a 'client' outside the set to whom the set members are responsible for the progress of the task or problem. Although each of us was working on real problems directly pertinent to our job responsibilities, we did not have a client. We were our own clients using the set for our own purposes even though there would be a benefit to the organization for those of us concerned with pursuing tasks based on the organization. An example of this was taking a postgraduate management development programme from an interesting and rather novel idea through to successful validation and implementation. The novel idea was the use of action learning as the major vehicle for learning! Hence the desire for some of us to do action learning if we were going to prescribe it for those embarking on our courses.

Second, and in our view most importantly, we decided to work without a set adviser. We would do that task ourselves. We will look at the implications below.

Third, we set up our particular group voluntarily. Whilst all working in the same organization the set was not formally recognized by the organization. We met in our own time. We were a self-facilitated and independent set at the same time.

Since this initial set we have continued to be members of self-facilitated sets and initiated them in organizations. It is from these experiences that we draw our ideas for their successful operation.

What is Needed for a Self-facilitated Set?

Potential set members

Personal commitment is important for a set member in a traditional set. That commitment is even more important in the early stages of a self-facilitated set. Drawing upon Heron's (1989) modes of facilitation, this form of action learning is at the autonomous end of the spectrum where set members share responsibility for the maintenance of the set, its procedures and processes (see Chapter 6). There is no facilitator to take responsibility when the set is detracting from its purpose. Each set member in a self-facilitated set *shares* the responsibility otherwise vested in a facilitator.

When creating a new self-facilitated set the potential set members need commitment that is and remains voluntary. We do this by ensuring that the first meeting is a 'taster'. The first meeting works as a set but we are clear it is open to anyone to say that it is not what they anticipated and that they may choose not to come to subsequent meetings. This is similar to facilitated sets. A potential set member should not feel obliged to join a set just because it has met or feel any group pressure to continue. It may mean that the set is stillborn. If there are sufficient who wish to continue then the basis for real commitment has been identified.

Drawing upon the initial Brighton set (McGill *et al*, 1990) we saw that:

> For each person, personal commitment to the set and the way it worked was a priority. Being at the set was very important compared to other activities associated with our work. This generated a feeling of protectiveness towards the time of the set. Something that required so much effort to protect and sustain could not fail to attain significance.

Procedures

At the first meeting of a set basic procedures and ground rules need to be agreed. They may be modified at subsequent meetings to suit the set. These include:

- *Life expectancy of the set*. The set agrees the overall length of time for which it will hold a cycle of meetings. It may be six or nine months or a year, after which time the set reviews its progress. (See Chapter 6 for review processes.) We would not recommend that a set begins to meet without determining a review meeting at the end of the agreed cycle of meetings.
- *Review meeting*. The set may determine to end after the review meeting, continue for a further period and/or add to or alter the membership. The review stage is an important learning process. The finite period of meeting also provides a limit at which all set members can make a judgement about whether they continue or not.
- *Frequency of meetings*. This is dependent on the needs of members. However, meetings once every two to five weeks enable set members to maintain momentum and to fulfil actions between set meetings.
- *Set numbers and duration of set meetings*. There is a relationship between the number of members in a set and the duration of each set meeting. These are usually two to three hours dependent upon the number of set members. A small set of three or four can get through business in two hours. Five or six members will need three hours. We do not recommend sets below four unless there is a degree of action learning experience amongst members. Occasionally, the set may agree a full day meeting to give set members more time, to review the set process and to celebrate the set!

- *Time allocation at meetings*. This is usually equally divided after allowing sufficient time for informalities (how we are feeling today) and common business (diaries for subsequent meetings). The set may agree that a member have more time if there is a felt need.
- *Time-keeping and note-taking*. Without a facilitator these key functions need to be allocated. Time-keeping is necessary to prevent time drifting, with the effect of reducing another set member's time. One person also needs to maintain a note of set member actions for circulation amongst the group so that recall is prompted by the note before and at the next set meeting.

An appreciation of how a self-facilitated set can work is conveyed in the extract below. This is an account of how the first Brighton self-facilitated set experienced being set members. The extract takes up the story after we had completed a cycle of meetings and a review. It gives a collective overview of what it felt like being in the set.

The initial Brighton self-facilitated set

We gained support from each other. Approval and disapproval were suspended. There was a sense of effort and fair exchange in the time, advice, attention of others, each received.

We confronted each other in a supportive way. No-one was to be *made* to face up to anything about themselves. The questions posed would enable an individual to reflect constructively on their situation. For example, one question posed to the first author was what would be the impact of a particularly taxing work programme upon his personal relationship with his partner, something he had unwittingly not considered. He had made assumptions as a man about the work overriding the partnership and the needs of and impact upon his partner. At about the same time he had been addressing his sexism and his relations with women, yet had not thought through that closest to him. The set highlighted the issue. That simple question certainly enabled a subjective confrontation to take place as well as reflecting upon and acting on sexism in the wider sense.

The questions could just be listened to and then thought about privately afterwards. The set always explored, 'What for? Is that really the best way? Is that really what you want?' The emphasis was on constructive discussion of alternative ways forward. Set members had different backgrounds and lives and the problems brought to the group were different. However there were so many threads in common, that the situation of the other was very real. A frequent comment referred to the realisation, 'that I am not alone in this organisation in terms of my concerns and ideas'.

Listening was one of the most important things we all did for each other. People became increasingly generous of their time and attention to others, realising that listening and learning are linked. It became clear that we were learning about ourselves and our tasks while listening to the others. Maybe it is what is at the heart of all support groups, and this action learning set was definitely a support group in Reg Revans' (1980) sense of 'comrades in adversity'. One of the set described this process as 'relieving oppressions'.

The climate of developing trust was the groundwork on which everything was laid. Set members who had been working colleagues yet strangers, often for some years, evolved a genuine intimacy once the set had established itself as open, non-competitive and non-threatening.

Caring as a form of positive reinforcement to each other was a key feature. The concern of others let us be kinder to ourselves. Often when exploring and analysing the self, we are only able to be critical. Being positive about ourselves seemed to require the participation of others. 'Caring for each other: this emerged slowly and was unexpected in its depth', as one of our set put it.

The set worked. It was effective. Tasks that seemed daunting initially progressed; objectives were achieved or reviewed. It cannot be too strongly emphasised that success at the task itself was part of the process that welded the set together and gave it purpose. The set was not just a talking shop. Working contracts were made and we all felt the obligation to meet them, meeting by meeting. They gave a clear sense of purpose. At the same time meeting or failing to meet the contract, was not the responsibility of the set, but of the individual. The contract was to help the person not the set. However the growing sense of loyalty to the group and its expectations often led the individual to do better for the set than they would for themselves.
(McGill et al, 1990).

Applications of Self-facilitated Sets

The self-facilitated set described above provides a useful example of how sets can be extended in organizations. As it happens we started as an independent set. Over a period of about three years it led to more independent sets being created, then the organization creating sets for course delivery purposes. There is an infinite variety of ways in which sets can be created in organizations with or without the organization's support.

We have chosen some applications to demonstrate the way in which self-facilitated sets can be used and to show that they may be used alongside facilitated sets.

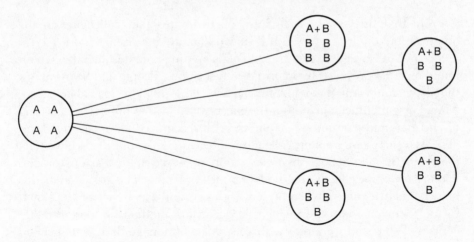

Key:
A = original set members
B = second stage new set members + an A

Figure 7.1 *Extending self-facilitated sets*

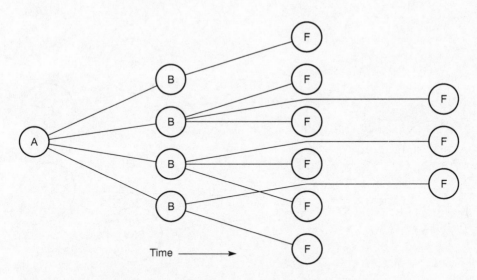

Time ⟶

Key:
A = the original set and its members as in Figure 7.1
B = self-facilitated sets initiated by set members from A
F = sets facilitated by set members from B

Figure 7.2 *Organizationally supported facilitated sets*

From that first set we each went on to invite other colleagues in the organization to join a new set. It is shown diagramatically in Figure 7.1.

The new sets were created by each of us inviting potential members to an initial meeting preceded by informal conversations. People had heard about the first set and wanted to join. Starting new sets seemed the logical next step. Not all new members stayed but the effect overall was to put action learning on the map in the organization and to get it recognized as an effective form of self-development amongst colleagues. The experience outlined above took place in a Business School, an organization interested in the learning process and in developing effective methods of student learning. The independent sets helped create a culture whereby staff with personal experience of sets began to use them on their courses as a key learning method for postgraduate courses. Those staff were now acting as set facilitators guiding managers on management development programmes, so the model in Figure 7.1 changed to that shown in Figure 7.2.

The above example shows how an organization can make effective use of limited resources and achieve development of its staff. We are not advocating that those responsible for staff/management development in organizations

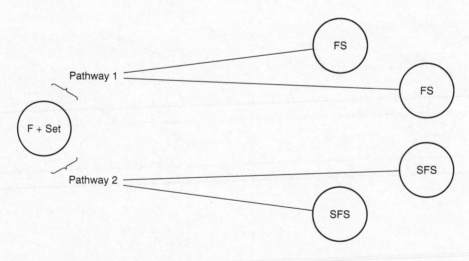

Key:
F = facilitator of the first set
FS = facilitated set
SFS = self-facilitated set

Figure 7.3 *Development with action learning: pathways*

leave their staff to start sets themselves as a cheap way of encouraging development of staff. However, the model can be adapted as in Figure 7.3 to organizations that take responsibility for using action learning as a part of their developmental repertoire.

In Figure 7.3 the organization appoints a set adviser who facilitates a set consisting of members with little experience of group facilitation who gain, over time, an understanding of the set process. Over a period of, say, one year those set members who are willing and who are confident of initiating a set move on to new sets consisting of staff who have been invited to join and who wish to become set members for their own development.

This second stage has two possible pathways. Pathway one is where the original set members become facilitators for the new sets. Pathway two is where original set members merely act as initiators and all members of the set

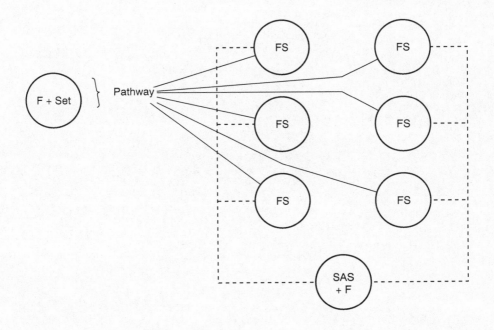

Key:
F = facilitator of the first set
FS = facilitated set
SAS = set advisers' set for the facilitators of new sets

Figure 7.4 *Support for internal facilitator*

move into self-facilitation mode. We recommend the latter when new set members have some experience of group work.

Both pathways require the initial resource of time of the set members in the set for the developmental process plus the costs of employing the set facilitator.

Finally, if the organization wishes the 'new' internal facilitators as in pathway one above to have their own support, the original set facilitator may act as set adviser to the facilitators, as in Figure 7.4.

PART II

DEVELOPING ACTION LEARNING SKILLS

Chapter 8

A Workshop for Introducing Action Learning

Our purpose in this chapter is to describe an approach to a workshop that conveys a real sense of what action learning is to potential users of the method before they fully commit themselves to working in action learning sets. An organization or group may decide that action learning may meet some of its needs and purposes. As advocates or consultants we have the task of convincing potential users of the advantages of using action learning.

We are addressing two potentially overlapping identifiable groups. The first are managers, trainers and staff developers, who may be considering using action learning for personal, managerial development of their staff. This group could also include educationalists and teachers who may wish to use action learning as a vehicle for learning in courses. The second potential group are those staff, managers and students who may be the participants in a set for their developmental and learning needs. The latter would also include those considering an independent set.

We believe that the most effective way to convey the potential value of action learning is to *do* it. We have found that those who wish to use action learning may have read about action learning, may have had action learning described to them but they may still remain sceptical because of an unfamiliarity with this way of working together. There are severe limitations to the verbal description of the process because the description lacks the key ingredient of people actually engaging together. *Doing* action learning overcomes these problems and gives them a real feel for the process – how it works for them.

Uses of the Workshop

This workshop method and approach can be used for the following purposes:

- To introduce participants to action learning as a vehicle for their personal and/or management development who are unaware of the process of action learning. Participants may then follow through with planned programmes of action learning sessions.
- As above but with the intention to follow the session with a programme of action learning that is self-facilitated, ie, without a set adviser (McGill *et al*, 1990). Here the set adviser models practice that is later emulated by all members.
- With participants who are familiar with action learning but who wish to become set advisers. The workshop gives participants the opportunity to observe the process of action learning.
- As a basis for 'cascading' in organizations. Once action learning becomes an organic part of the development of staff in an organization, the workshop can be used to introduce staff new to the method.

Workshop Benefits

The workshop conveys the nature of action learning. The method has the following advantages:

- Experimentation before commitment. The method acknowledges that participants at an introductory workshop may not yet have fully committed themselves to joining or starting a set. The participants can therefore obtain a close understanding of the process before fully committing themselves.
- Working with a large group of potential action learners. We are also frequently asked to introduce action learning to a significant number of people who may form more than one set. The workshop method enables us to reach a wide number of interested people. We have had as many as 40

engaged in this initial workshop but the more usual number is between 12 and 20 participants.

- Convey more accurately the *how* of action learning. The workshop enables potential action learners to get an idea and a feel of what it is like to be in a set. The key to action learning is in the process as well as what is dealt with at the set – the content. The process is about *how* a set works. An analogy might be learning about a new activity, say, cycling or swimming. You can read about it, have it described to you but it is not the same as doing it. Similarly with action learning – doing it makes all the difference to understanding and feeling what it is like to be a member of a set.

- The workshop method works. The method serves its purpose and engenders enthusiasm beyond that associated with merely having action learning described.

- Self-screening. The workshop has a benefit once action learning sets are created, for it means that there is a greater likelihood of the set(s) continuing and maintaining itself. 'Self-screening' can occur at the workshop stage. This is useful as it reduces the number of those who may join a set but subsequently decide that it is not really what they expected and then leave. When such early withdrawal from a set happens the numbers in the set may be reduced so that the set is no longer viable. This in turn can be dispiriting to the active and committed set members. A new set that has experienced the introductory workshop method is thus more likely to take off successfully, maintain its numbers and be effective for each individual and as a set.

- Cost effectiveness. The workshop is cost effective in reaching a wide number of potential users and ensures that the sets that are created are more likely to maintain their numbers and use the process of action learning more effectively and at an earlier stage. We have used the approach in universities, local authorities, companies, and at conferences and workshops. Participants have been managers, academics, administrators, students and self-support groups, the latter wanting to go further than just being support groups.

How the Introductory Workshop is Organized

The workshop has four phases which may be modified according to the time available. A full-day workshop will enable all phases below to be undertaken. It is possible to adapt the workshop to fit a minimum time of three hours. In this description we will assume a day for the workshop. The phases are as follows:

1) Introduction to action learning.
2) Concentric circles.
3) Practising action learning in sets.
4) Reflection and moving on.

In Phase 1 we aim to give a brief overview of the purpose of the day, a description of what action learning is, how it can be used and in what contexts. Phase 2, concentric circles, is the key to the workshop and the core activity that would be the basis of a workshop even with more limited time. This phase conveys to the whole workshop the nature of action learning through *doing* it. Phase 3, practising action learning in sets, gives all the participants a more direct experience of action learning by running sets concurrently for part of the workshop. Phase 4, reflection and moving on, enables all participants to review the workshop and reflect upon the potential of action learning. We will detail the activities within each phase. The phases

Prior briefing with the organization or sponsor

PHASE 1
Introduction to the day:
Purpose, structure and format

Working in Triads
Plenary debriefing and reflection on triads

PHASE 2
Concentric circles
Plenary reflection on the process
One-to-one reflection on the process

PHASE 3
Practising action learning in sets

PHASE 4
Workshop reflection

Moving on
Ending

Figure 8.1 *The phases of an introductory workshop*

are shown in Figure 8.1 which could form the basis for a workshop programme.

Phase 1: Introduction to action learning

This phase includes a description of what action learning is, how it can be used and in what contexts it is appropriate. Further, an outline of the structure and purpose of the workshop will enable participants to clarify what they will wish to achieve.

It is important that the facilitator of the workshop undertakes a prior briefing with the clients to determine the background of those attending, including their familiarity with working in groups, participative forms of learning and working together and the skills that are a particular emphasis in action learning.

The workshop starts with introductions and a useful warm-up activity that is appropriate for the group. The warm-up is designed to create an environment that contributes to developing trust and support. The activity will ensure that everybody gets to know each other, their first names, roles (if appropriate), their expectations of the workshop and something that the group do not know about 'me' that 'I' am willing to share with the group. This is just one format for starting the workshop. There are many others. This is followed with an outline of the purpose and structure of the day. Here it is emphasized that we will be experiencing individually and collectively action learning and related activities. To undertake the experiential activities effectively requires an atmosphere of confidentiality and trust in a safe environment. Through the remainder of this chapter we aim to convey the kinds of conditions which facilitators and participants can follow to ensure those requirements. Each phase and activity needs to convey the conditions for creating safety, confidentiality and trust appropriate to that activity.

We follow the brief warm-up with a small-group activity known as 'triads'. For participants with little experience of interpersonal skills training or group activity we find this is a valuable entry to action learning work, enabling each participant to present an issue with another giving attentive listening. Triads take about one and a half hours and are very effective in introducing participants to the process of enabling individuals to work to some purpose on their issues or problem as well as heightening participants' sensitivity to the skills of presenting, enabling and observing which occur in an action learning set. The triad process is a 'safe' activity because, as its name suggests, three people work together for the designated period before working in a larger group in Phase 2. The triad is a stepping stone to the next phase as it enables participants to use and acknowledge skills in a small group as well as creating the conditions for trust to be engendered.

Participants in triads frequently say how unusual it is to have such undivided attention. To be really listened to as a presenter is an important ingredient of action learning as is the complementary capacity to listen on the part of the enabler.

The workshop participants are each given a written description of the triad activity as well as having it described by the facilitator. (The description is shown below.) Participants are divided into groups of three (or four where there is not a multiple of three). The groups can be self-selecting with a suggestion that participants work with those whom they least know or do not know. Alternatively the facilitator can with agreement count round the group to divide into groups. Sometimes, this 'random' approach makes it easier for participants who are little known to each other. They are then invited to engage in the process set out below.

It is essential to agree ground rules for the activity before the activity commences. Confidentiality is the most significant. By confidentiality we mean that each participant in the triad agrees that the content of each other person's issue and their feelings will not be disclosed outside the triad. This agreement encourages trust and greater disclosure. The participants in the triad are also asked to do their own time-keeping to ensure all have the opportunity of each role. The times given are broad indicators. A triad may find that one or two of their number may require more time to consider their issue, in which case they can negotiate the allocation of time between them. Participants when observers are also asked to give specific feedback. This feedback is given within the triad group and is confidential to the members of the triad.

Triads: task/problem/issue resolution

Divide into groups in the following roles:

Presenter
You are to think of a task/problem/issue that you face in your role at work and discuss it with one of the group. Try to be brief and specific. The 'task', 'problem' or 'issue' should be of *real* concern to you.

Enabler
You are to help the presenter with his or her 'problem' by trying to get

---

the presenter to think through his or her issues. Ask open questions (How do you know? What does this mean?). The object is to enable the presenter to define or redefine the problem/issue and their relationship to it in specific terms for the *presenter* to take some steps towards solving it. Try to focus on what can be done *by* the presenter – not what others ought to do. Some helpful questions may include:

- It sounds as though you are feeling . . .
- How does that make you feel . . .
- What do you think is really going on . . .
- What do you think would happen if . . .
- Do you think that . . .
- How would you know if . . .
- What could you do . . .
- How can you . . .

Observer

The observer listens to what is being *said*. You observe the verbal interaction and consider what questions/responses were more/less helpful in enabling the presenter to move forward his or her issue. The observer also listens to/senses what the *feelings* of the presenter are in relation to their issue.

Finally, the observer also listens to/senses what the presenter has *invested* (or not) in the issue. What is the presenter's *will, commitment* or *motivation* toward the issue and its possible resolution?

Further points the observer may wish to consider include:

- is the enabler providing solutions for the presenter?
- is the presenter focusing on what they can do?
- is the presenter avoiding resolving the problem?
- is the presenter's proposed action specific enough?

Take 20–25 minutes between presenter and enabler. After the session and a pause, the presenter and enabler convey how the experience was for them. The observer then gives feedback for 5 minutes to the 'enabler' on how their behaviour aided the presenter, followed by 5 minutes to the presenter, and then the presenter and 'enabler' may wish to add their comments. Change roles in order that each person can take the role of enabler and presenter.

During the triad activity the facilitator may go round some of the groups and give feedback from observation that may not have been already covered by the observer to the presenter and enabler.

At the end of the activity, when all participants have experienced each role, the workshop participants are invited into a plenary circle to reflect on what they have gained from the activity and how it felt doing the activity. Each person should be given time to convey their thoughts and feelings. The facilitator can draw on the reflection to make comparisons with the process of action learning.

The round of reflection is useful to enable participants to understand the value of the process of the triad, the skills that are being harnessed and that the activity embraces some of the skills and roles that are found in action learning. As presenter, the participants gain experience in having specific time for an issue or problem that is relevant and of concern to them. The presenter may be very clear about the issue being raised or start with only a tentative idea or a feeling about something; either way they are given undivided attention to their issue. The key here is that the enabler is able to attend to the presenter without having a vested interest in the presenter's issues. The enabler gains experience in the act of attending to another person and is given feedback on their skills in listening, questioning, empathizing, challenging and confronting. Participants state how rare it is to get feedback on their use of these skills; they also convey in the plenary reflections how difficult it is not to try to provide the presenter with solutions! As observers, participants gain experience in a role which is rarely exercised in this form. In normal circumstances of interaction with others they are not usually 'detached' from the interaction.

Following the plenary reflection using triads we can now move to the central phase.

Phase 2: Concentric circles

This phase conveys to the whole workshop the nature of action learning through *doing* and experiencing it. This is the key to the workshop and the core activity that would be the basis of a workshop even with more limited time.

This phase commences with a verbal and, if helpful, a flip chart description of the way in which the concentric circles work and how participants can prepare themselves for the activity. The concentric circles consist of an inner circle of participants who work as an action learning set with a set adviser (the facilitator) and an outer circle of participants acting as observers of the action learning process taking place in the inner circle. The concentric circles are shown in Figure 8.2.

Figure 8.2 *Introducing action learning with concentric circles*

The inner circle is for the 'set' with a spare chair left vacant. The outer circle is for observers of the process and content. Participants as observers in the outer circle have the opportunity to take the chair when appropriate.

At this point it may be helpful to explain the reasons for using the circles method. Action learning requires to be experienced in order for each participant to get near to understanding its potentiality. If there are more participants than can be accommodated in a single set the use of circles can enable some of the participants to experience working directly in a set whilst the other participants can observe the process.

The participants are then asked if some will volunteer to work in the inner circle. Four to six volunteers are invited from the whole group who will form the 'set' with the facilitator of the workshop as set adviser. Volunteers are asked to think of an important, unresolved but real issue/problem/opportunity that has no obvious solution, which they are willing to talk through in the 'set' and with the outer circle of participants observing the process. Depending on time, the volunteers are also informed that we may only be able to take one or two of the 'set'.

Those who form the outer circle are asked to observe the content of the set discussion and, more importantly to observe the *process*. The content is the presenter's issue or problem. The process is what is happening in the set whilst the set is dealing with the issue – the *how* of action learning. The prior triad session provides a useful introduction to the role of observers in this session.

The volunteer set members can also be asked if they are willing to receive personal feedback from a participant who is acting as an observer in the outer circle. As facilitator, it is usual in inviting this additional form of feedback to suggest that the set member requests someone from the outer circle. That person may be someone they know or do not know but feel comfortable with. All observers then observe and make notes of the process, content and some observers additionally observe one person in particular in the set. It is emphasized prior to the action learning activity that the observer will give the feedback to the set member on a one-to-one basis privately after the plenary feedback on the whole process, providing a safer environment for the set member to receive feedback.

Two circles of chairs are formed for the 'set' and observers. In the inner circle an additional chair is left for any of the observers in the outer circle to occupy, for a moment only, to pose a question about content or to convey a process observation that may enable the 'set' to progress. The vacant chair is a useful device for it usually commits the interest of observers without losing sight of their main role. We will return to this type of intervention later.

The set then proceeds like a normal set. Ideally two facilitators run the workshop, one of whom will take the role of set adviser in the inner circle and model the role of set adviser as outlined in Chapter 6. The other facilitator joins the outer circle as one of the process observers. If there is only one facilitator, she should take the role of set adviser. In this chapter we only emphasize those particular tasks for the set adviser that enable the set to operate in this 'unusual' context.

The set adviser will aim to relax the volunteer set members who may initially feel some natural anxiety about being in the middle and under observation. Our experience is that once we get going that concern reduces significantly. Again a warm-up is beneficial to allay that concern and also help the forming of the set. One particular activity here that does not take too much time is called, 'Trauma, trivia and joy' and is set out below. This is a very useful activity for it enables the members of the set to convey how they are feeling with an informal immediacy.

Trauma, trivia and joy (adapted, with thanks to John Southgate)

Each person in the group is asked to convey briefly an event or incident, one of which could be termed a trauma, another a trivia, and one a joy that has happened to them in the last day or so. Each member of the set

---

takes a turn describing their events, including the set adviser who may start and therefore model the activity.

There is no discussion of the events. Other set members usually convey their empathy and feelings with the occasional word or feeling, the effect of which is to create a warm and supportive atmosphere, relax the set members and help the set to get to know each other a little. Set members are asked not to invent events if they have not actually occurred. If a set member has just a joy and trivia that is fine. If a set member wishes not to be included in this activity and 'pass' that is also legitimate. Most participants find the activity light and energizing.

Moreover, the activity may trigger an issue that a set member wishes to address and/or the event may unwittingly become a key part of the issue.

The activity will take about 5 to 15 minutes depending upon the numbers participating. It is important not to rush an individual but to convey the idea that it is a brief 'warm-up' to get us going.

With the warm-up completed, set members are then asked to describe in cameo form the issue that they would like to bring to the set. This is an important moment. As set adviser it is necessary to remind the set members that we will only have time for one person's issue or two at the most. Asking each person to convey the issue they would like to bring to the group is important in two ways. First, it conveys to the set and the outer circle of observers the range of issues that the volunteer members of the set would like to bring to the set. This immediately conveys to all present what individuals consider they could bring to the set that could be useful for them. In terms of conveying the potential of action learning, hearing examples of what could be brought to a set is instructive. Second, hearing the issues that could come before the set helps the set members to make up their minds on which person's issue they would like to consider. A set member may decide that another's is more pertinent than the one they raised. Describing the issues also conveys some significant openness and courage to all those listening. Examples of issues that volunteer set members might bring forward could be:

- organizing my time over the day (week or any period) at work;
- balancing my priorities of work with the rest of my life;
- deciding whether to register for a postgraduate qualification;
- how can I ensure that my 0.5 job share stays at 0.5 and does not become a near full-time job?

- being new to the post how can I get support without conveying the impression that I am not 'up' to the job?

Note that the issues are critical to the person conveying them. What is brought to the volunteer set will depend on the degree of trust and therefore safety the volunteer feels towards the people in the circles. It is appropriate for the facilitator to emphasize that volunteers only bring issues that they feel safe to bring to this unusual situation, particularly in organizational settings. Once a normal set is in operation the safety is usually enhanced and the trust enables more openness and disclosure of more sensitive and personal issues.

It is important that the set adviser lets the set members come to agreement about whose issue is considered. In the event of stalemate when the set members cannot agree whose issue should be taken the set adviser may have to resolve it. In our experience this has only happened once. At the suggestion of the set adviser it was amicably resolved with the toss of a coin! This, incidentally, ensured that the set adviser was not steering what should be discussed and who would bring their issue, only the process of moving on.

Guidelines for the 'set' members
Here we give only a brief indication of the main guidelines for a set in the workshop as full details are given elsewhere (see Chapters 2, 4, 5 and 6). Also, when facilitating a set in the workshop, we aim to minimize the verbal description of the process.

Once the set has agreed who will volunteer, the set adviser re-emphasizes briefly that the presenter has 40 minutes in total as their time – the initial, say, 10 minutes of which is for the presenter to convey her thoughts on the issue to the set as listeners. Following her introduction to her issue, the set members and adviser can ask questions that seek to clarify what she as presenter has conveyed and to check out their understanding of her thoughts and feelings. The set adviser also emphasizes that the questioning should be supportive of the presenter in enabling the latter to focus on their issue. The interaction should be supportive yet challenging for the presenter. The interaction is not an interrogation!

The aim of the set is to enable the presenter to reach her own solutions, not for the other set members to present their solutions to her. This is the key to the whole process of interaction between the presenter and colleagues in the set. This enables the presenter to begin *taking* responsibility for her actions.

During the time taken by the presenter, she may say something like, 'I ought to do this because . . .'. It is often very helpful to ask the presenter what she means by 'ought'. This enables the presenter to distinguish between 'oughts' and 'wants' and to clarify their thoughts and feelings on an issue. Complementary to this is drawing the attention of set members to the danger of 'oughts' hidden in questions that may be designed to be helpful to the presenter but are actually solutions they consciously or unconsciously wish to impose on the presenter.

Further details of the operation of the set are given in Chapters 4 and 5. As facilitator of the introductory session and as acting set adviser it is important to convey to the 'set' and the observers just sufficient information to get started. Otherwise there is a danger of the facilitator doing the very thing he or she wishes to avoid, namely talking about action learning as opposed to giving participants experience of the process of doing it. The above indicators by the set adviser are therefore the minimum to get the set working and avoid inadequate outcomes in terms of the learning about the potential effectiveness of action learning.

As the volunteer presenter nears the end of her issue she is asked to convey how she would like to take her issue forward following the meeting and possibly to 'contract' with another person on the workshop to ensure action occurs. The contract is simply an agreement to contact the other person within a given period of time (say, a month) to convey the presenter's progress on action she agreed in the set. Undertaking a 'contract' of this kind replaces the usual arrangement set members have between one meeting and the next – a crucial aspect of set activity which the workshop cannot replicate.

One or two volunteers will have taken about one hour. It is important to judge the total length of time so that there is sufficient range of the process without losing the attention of the observers.

Reflection on the process by the participants
Before completion of Phase 2 it is necessary for the workshop to reflect on the process of the inner circle or set. The workshop participants then form one circle. Following a short break, it is important to enable the inner circle 'set' members to start by conveying their initial feelings about the process. We usually suggest that the presenter(s) is last in this part of the reflection. The presenter should also have the option to opt out of this, as should all the inner circle, if they wish to. This is simply to recognize that the set members and particularly the presenter may well have become very engaged in the process and have feelings and emotions that they wish to gradually lighten but are not yet ready to reflect upon.

Going round, each person in the outer circle who observed the process then relates their description of the process. It is in this reflection stage that participants gain their understanding of what action learning is really about. There is a tendency for the observers from the outer circle to re-engage with the content as opposed to conveying their feedback about the process observed and what was significant in that process. It is unhelpful for the presenter to have the content 'opened up' after she has agreed her actions. The only exception here is if a reference to the content is necessary to make a point about process.

The facilitator may wish to follow up the process discussion by highlighting the main points on flip chart for reflection. Following the plenary reflection on the process observed by the outer circle, those observers who additionally observed, by prior agreement, a set member, give feedback in confidence to that person on a one-to-one basis.

Phase 3: Practising action learning in sets

Phase 3 gives all the participants an experience of action learning by running sets for part of the workshop concurrently. This part of the workshop will depend upon the number of participants and facilitators and the experience of the participants. Sets are created with five or six participants per set. Participants can be facilitated with set advisers if there are enough for the number of sets required or there can be a combination of facilitated and self-facilitated sets.

Facilitators and participants in sets in this part of the workshop will again be constrained by time. The same process as for the inner circle in Phase 2 will be applied. One or two volunteers will be invited following an appropriate warm-up and brief summaries of each person's issue described to the set. The major difference in this stage is that all participants are engaged as direct participants in the sets without external observers. In this phase all participants integrate the role of observation into their role as set members.

Timing of the set is left to the set adviser with an indication of when the sets will come back into plenary for the final reflection. Time available will determine whether there are one or more presenters within each set. Ten minutes or so is appropriate at the end of the set session to enable each person in the set to convey within the set how the process felt for them.

Phase 4: Reflection: gains from the day and moving on

With Phases 1 to 3 completed, the workshop can conclude with an overall reflection on the day. The purpose of this stage is to enable participants to reflect on what they have gained and learned individually and collectively.

Before engaging in the reflection it is appropriate to use a short period for any factual clarification by participants of any aspects of the action learning process and the potential uses of action learning.

How can this important stage be organized for maximum effect for each participant? Participants can be asked a range of questions that enable them to reflect upon the workshop with a view to its relevance and future use for them. Working individually, then in pairs, participants could be asked to reflect upon the following questions:

- What have I gained/learned from the workshop today:
  - for myself
  - in my work (if applicable)
  - in relation to my colleagues and friends?
- What personal changes will I undertake/implement myself and with colleagues?
- Where do I/we go from here?
- What actions am I going to take:
  - from my work in the 'set' (if the participant had this opportunity)
  - to enable me to influence the forming of a set and/or create a set?

The responses to the above questions will depend upon the nature of the relationship of the participants at the workshop. For example, if the workshop is organizationally based, the focus may be on a structured response to the creation of sets for staff and management development purposes as outlined in Chapter 2. The manager responsible for staff development can then move on to devising a programme of development using action learning sets with the knowledge of those who wish to engage in this approach.

If the workshop has been organized round individual responses to attending then the questions may require participants to assess how they may get sets going in their work, amongst voluntary groups or with colleagues and friends. Sets may also be based on gender or ethnicity to enable participants to work on issues common to them.

Following the pairs work, participants can then share their ideas and feelings in a final plenary. This ensures a cross-fertilization of the ideas and can act as an energizer for each participant. The workshop can then conclude with an appropriate round such as a single phrase which sums up the day for each of the participants.

Chapter 9

Skills Development: The Basics

The purpose of this and the next chapter is to enable set members to consider the interpersonal skills they use that make for effective working of the set for themselves and for other members of the set. Facilitators may wish to use some of the activities to focus on a skill that could be developed or enhanced by members of the set. Chapters 9 and 10 are also intended for action learning practitioners to reflect on their current use of the skills. We would like to emphasize that these chapters are to be used as a resource when particular set members and facilitators wish to give attention to a skill(s) that they wish to practise and/or reflect upon.

Groups: Working Together

Group working calls for good basic interpersonal skills which until recently have not been addressed in schools and post-school education. It has been suggested (Egan, 1976; Heron, 1989) that in British and American cultures we do not give much explicit attention to the development of our interpersonal skills. We would endorse that general view. Egan (1976) stated it this way:

> when I suggest to some people that they may profit from involvement in a . . . group, they respond (at least non-verbally) as if I had asked them to take a trip to Antarctica. They don't feel prepared for a group experience because their lives have been devoid of similar experiences.

The educational experiences of most of us in our culture will have centred round the teacher with the occasional 'group discussion', but we are rarely asked or enabled to be personal in a group or to share ourselves with any degree of openness.

Heron's (1989) view, in a UK context, is that we tend to lack basic human skills:

> skills in handling (our) own feelings, skills in interacting with other persons, skills in self-direction and collective decision-making.

We would agree with these statements with a reservation – that we have and try to use the skills but that they are not consciously developed.

Until a few years ago, although we have been called teachers, lecturers and tutors, we had not paid much attention to the development of our interpersonal skills, and if asked to engage in such an activity to explore and enhance those skills we would have found a way of avoiding the situation as potentially embarrassing and very exposing. At the same time, we as tutors would be asking students in higher education to work in groups on assignments or projects, somehow expecting them to do it without doing it ourselves in other contexts or modelling effective group practice with students. Similarly, we would expect managers to work in groups assuming they found group work straightforward.

Our personal experience was a common one in higher education and in many other organizations. Developed skills in this area were the preserve of some of the 'caring' professions like counselling, therapy and social work. The notion that such skills were the preserve of these professions only deepened prejudice about their use in other contexts. Fortunately the enhancement of these basic skills is now seen as a prerequisite for personal effectiveness as managers, teachers, lecturers, retailers and in most working (and personal) situations. As colleagues in work we can make for better working relationships by enhancing these skills.

For a number of years now we have believed, and put into practice our belief, that interpersonal skills and personal effectiveness in groups are very important. Few of us live and work in isolation; so much of our experience in work and life rests upon being effective in the presence of and with other people. Having knowledge about something may be useless if we cannot convey, act, interrelate, in a manner that is effective for the purpose.

Groups that are facilitated inappropriately or insensitively can, partly because of the facilitator's lack of skills training, actually compound the difficulty for participants. Shock stories then move on to the rumour track and frighten off more people from group-based work.

De-mystification about how sets work has been a major purpose of this book. Action learning is a particular form of group working that is highly structured and supportive of participant set members. The structured way in which the set works is particularly important in the early life of a set when participants may be apprehensive about working in groups. The way the group is intended to work in an action learning set creates a very supportive group environment. Yet with practice and some continuity it can be a challenging and non-collusive environment beneficial to its members. Chapter 4 describes the basic processes of a set meeting. If these procedures are broadly adhered to then the set can begin to work safely. Set members may like to refer to Chapter 5 to complement the skills addressed in this and the next chapter.

Interpersonal Skills

This review of interpersonal skills is designed to enable readers to focus on their current interpersonal style and possibly modify it in order to enhance their interpersonal effectiveness. We distinguish between basic and additional interpersonal skills. Listening, reflection and disclosure are basic skills. These basic skills provide the foundation for the effective use of higher level skills. The latter include the expression of emotion and empathy. Using these additional skills effectively produces a rapport among set members which enables giving and receiving of feedback. In terms of the action focus of action learning, set members can effectively focus and specify those actions the presenter wishes to take.

The remainder of this and the next chapter will address the following skills:

Basic Skills:
Effective use of interpersonal skills
Listening
Reflecting back
Disclosure

Additional Skills (Chapter 10):
Management of emotion
Empathy
Giving and receiving feedback
Shoulds and oughts
Generalizations
Specifying actions

We will continue to use the term 'presenter' for the set member conveying her issues to the set. The listener is any set member or the facilitator. We will also, where appropriate, use an example drawn from experience, of a woman as presenter conveying issues which are important to her, to other set members and a facilitator. We will refer to this example in the text to develop the significance of the skills in use.

Effective Use of Interpersonal Skills

We bring a variety of interpersonal skills to social situations of which action learning is one form. Each interpersonal skill when enacted has three parts. First, the awareness or perception by me of what is happening – the knowing. Second, my ability to communicate – the doing. Third, my assertiveness with which I convey it – the will or guts to deliver my message.

By awareness or perception, the knowing, we mean:

- Being in touch with myself. I know what's going on inside me especially what I am feeling at the moment. If a friend says to me, 'Why are you so angry?' and I reply, 'Who's angry?', I am not realizing that I am angry. Getting feedback from a set can help us get in touch with ourselves.
- Being in touch with others. A good listener picks up clues such as the use of a presenter's language, his non-verbal behaviour and how that relates to what he is saying. In the process the set member gets an understanding of what's going on inside another's world.
- Being in touch with what's happening between two people. In a set I can listen to the interaction and understand what each is saying and/or communicating.
- Being in touch with what's happening in a group. This is more complicated but brings the above 'in touch' skills to a set.
- Being aware of strengths and weaknesses. I am aware through attentive listening where people have more of one skill than another. We tend to see more of our weaknesses rather than our strengths. Feedback can help us see the latter.

By ability to communicate, the doing, we mean:

- Attending to the other person. Just being with another person – really with them in terms of our non-verbal behaviour as well as what we say – is important.
- Being willing to be self-disclosing means that I am setting up the first

condition of reciprocal interaction. Negatively, if I am unwilling to be open about myself I am unlikely to encourage others.

- Active listening, that is listening to the non-verbal messages of the presenter.
- Non-verbal messages can confirm or reinforce what is said, but be careful: they can also confuse.

By assertiveness, the will or guts, we mean:

- Expressing my needs, wants, opinions, beliefs and feelings in direct, honest and appropriate ways.
- Conveying my own rights without violating the rights of others.
- Taking responsibility for myself and what I say, 'owning' my needs, feelings, etc. For example, if I say to someone, 'You've upset me', this is aggressive rather than assertive because I am placing responsibility for the anger on that person rather than owning my own feeling of being upset, in contrast to, 'I'm upset because . . .'.
- Owning my feelings means that I cannot be criticized for having them – they just are.
- That an empathic response is more likely than a 'should' response so that; 'I feel upset' is likely to be met by, 'I wonder if you feel upset because . . .', rather than, 'You should pull yourself together'.

Assertive behaviour

Assertive behaviour is contrasted with unassertive or passive and aggressive behaviour.

If I behave unassertively where I do not express my needs or express them in a self-effacing or passive way, there are likely to be consequences for me. In the short term I might be more acceptable, reduce anxieties I may have about not being disagreeable and even gain some admiration from others for letting them get their own way. In the longer term I will allow others to take advantage of me, lose the respect of others, and possibly explode at some point.

If I behave aggressively I will stand up for my rights by violating the rights of others. I will ignore or dismiss their needs, wants, opinions, feelings and beliefs and express my own in inappropriate ways. In the short term I may release tension, have a sense of power and have admiration from others not affected by my aggression. In the longer term I may be the recipient of retaliatory action, tend to blame others, create an atmosphere of distrust, isolate myself and lose the support of and rapport with others.

The action learning set is conducive to an assertive mode in that the process is designed to give the presenter the opportunity to express her needs, wants, opinions, beliefs and feelings in direct, honest and appropriate ways. Enabling the presenter in an action learning set to have that opportunity is achieved by other set members being aware of what is happening in the group, having the ability to communicate what they mean and the assertiveness to convey their message appropriately. Egan (1976) has stated; 'Assertiveness is the ability to take *reasonable* risks' (emphasis in the original). In the context of a set it enables the presenter to work on her issues effectively, supportively and without collusion. Set members are encouraged to acknowledge each other's rights as well as having equal time for expression of their own.

Listening

When an action learning set is working effectively as a set, in particular for the person presenting, the whole set is *really* listening. We regard this as one of the basic skills brought to a set. It is a basic skill but probably the most important upon which the remainder of the skills we address in this chapter depend. By listening we mean the ability of the listener to 'capture and understand the messages [presenters] communicate, whether these messages are transmitted verbally or nonverbally, clearly or vaguely' (Egan, 1990).

People spend much of their lives listening, unless they have an impediment in their hearing. It is a very familiar activity. However, despite the significance of listening, people experience *not* being listened to. We still are surprised by the commentary from a set member that has this refrain:

> It really is a luxury to be listened to, really listened to. In my work I can go through the week with colleagues without them knowing what I am feeling or thinking. I suspect I am the same with them.

or

> This is the only place where I have the space to be listened to. No one listens to each other in the department.

Set members when reviewing how their set has worked over a cycle of meetings refer to how affirming it is to be listened to by other set members. Affirmation of the person expresses that person's essential worth as a human being just as the opposite behaviour can undermine that essential worth. This is easy to say, but there is a tendency for us to lose what a person has said because we may listen very inattentively. We may lose a significant part of what is being said simply because the act of verbal communication is itself complex even though we take it for granted. See what happens when A communicates with B in the example below.

Losing the message

A has a feeling or an idea she wishes to express.
A finds words which may or may not accurately reflect her idea.
A transmits her message.
B receives physical sounds and visual signals and decodes them.
B relates the message to her own feelings and ideas, may make judgements, create arguments, perhaps while A is still speaking, and may miss part of the message.
At this point B may decode incorrectly for all sorts of reasons:

- lack of understanding;
- parts of the message are lost;
- confusion caused by conflict between verbal and non-verbal information;
- having a negative or positive 'fix'.

By the word 'fix' we mean the tendency for selective listening – only hearing what we want to hear. We often evaluate the listener as they are speaking, eg, when a politician of a different persuasion to ourselves speaks, we may 'switch off' and only hear what we want to hear. Similarly with a politician of our own persuasion! The listener evaluates the message as it is transmitted, judges it and rejects or accepts it without critical analysis. Whilst this is common it can lead to poor interpersonal relations in work, in relationships and certainly would be less than useful in an action learning set.
There are many ways in which the message can be lost!

How can we reduce this loss of what is transmitted? We can do so by *attending* to the presenter, suspending our responses to enable us to reflect on the presenter's message, and checking internally that we are with the presenter in a non-judgemental way.

Attending to the presenter

Attending refers to the way in which we can be *with* our presenter (in the context of a set meeting) both physically and psychologically. A feature of a set meeting where listening by the whole set is happening is the sense of the presenter being attended to. By this is meant the quality of the attention the other set members are giving to the presenter. Egan (1990) has characterized this with the useful acronym *SOLER* to convey the minimum requirements for a listener (set member and facilitator) to attend to a presenter.

S – face the presenter *Squarely*, that is with a posture that conveys involvement, reflects the presenter in a positive manner and indicates that you wish to be with the presenter. This is not meant to be in a threatening manner but just one that suggests you wish to be with them – inclining towards the presenter. The posture shows that you are not distracted.

O – adopting an *Open* posture. Crossed arms and legs may convey a closed stance towards the presenter. Such a posture may not necessarily mean that you are closed toward the presenter, but it may convey it non-verbally to her. The key question to ask is to what extent is my physical posture conveying an openness and availability to the presenter?

L – at times it is possible to *Lean* toward the presenter in a way which suggests engagement. We can see this when observing people in pubs and restaurants leaning forward, leaning back or away.

E – maintain *Eye* contact with the presenter. This is a useful indicator of involvement which does not have to be continuous to be effective. It does not mean 'eyeball to eyeball' either!

R – be relatively *Relaxed* in your behaviour. This means not being physically distracting or fidgety. It also means being comfortable with the presenter so that your body can convey non-verbal expression.

A commitment to listening to the presenter, utilizing *SOLER*, ensures authenticity. Contriving a physical stance will convey messages that are counter-productive for the presenter. Negative or uncomfortable messages might include staring, getting too squared up so that it becomes threatening, looking out of a window continually or tapping a pencil on a table! Being aware of the effect of your physical and emotional presence is the key. *SOLER* is useful to convey the basic features of attending. To the reader unfamiliar with the approach it may appear that to adopt the features could suggest a lack of genuineness or manipulation. It is designed rather to highlight what we all do naturally when we are authentically attending.

Active listening

Effectively attending to the presenter means that set members are in a position to listen carefully to what the presenter is saying verbally and non-verbally. Egan (1990) expresses active or complete listening as involving four things:

> first, observing and reading the [presenter's] non-verbal behaviour – posture, facial expressions, movement, tone of voice, and the like; second, listening to and understanding the [presenter's] verbal messages; third, listening to the whole person in the context of the social settings of life; fourth, tough-minded listening.

In relation to non-verbal behaviour it is important to recognize that we are still listening to presenters in a way that deepens our understanding of what they are trying to convey. It is helpful in forming an overall picture of where the presenter is. It is inappropriate to fix on an expression of non-verbal behaviour and then to create a total impression from that single piece of information.

Listening to and understanding the presenter's verbal messages are part of the whole picture. At this point the listener does not form her responses to the presenter but listens.

Engaging in the attentive behaviours described by *SOLER* will enhance the development of the skill of creative listening. An example would be where a presenter is telling what it is like for her, working in an office where there is a manager continuously baiting her for not adopting the norms of the office, which include late working in a predominately male work force. The listener may have some views about how he would cope in such an environment. For example, he may think, 'I could cope with that' or, 'It would not be a problem for me'. But if he listens to his own thoughts on coping, he may detract from how she is thinking, feeling and being in *her* environment. The key is for our listener to 'put aside' his own responses to her situation and listen from the presenter's standpoint – where she is coming from. As we shall see below, even when the listener responds, it is necessary to work with where she is and not give his own solutions to her predicament. Any responses should empower her to deal with her situation in a manner that is enabling for her.

Our listener will, if effective, place himself (as far as is possible as a man) in her context. That is, he will endeavour to understand what it is like to be a woman in a mostly male environment, to tackle a prevailing norm that she feels oppressed by. Rather than get trapped in his own contextual picture, what is her picture that he needs to understand to enable her to deal with it?

In this way he will be endeavouring to get into her social context – how working life is for her.

Tough-minded listening requires that our listener places himself in the frame of the presenter so that he really understands where she is coming from. It also means that he picks up what is perhaps being distorted by the presenter. For example, our presenter may be talking about going for a promotion in the organization and how she is well qualified for it. However, she is also conveying less explicitly through her voice tone, demeanour and some of her words that she may feel that she is not confident to do the job if promoted. This is turn may affect her will to apply for the post. It is for the listener to pick up this inconsistency and hold it until it is appropriate to offer it as an observation.

Hearing, active and passive listening

Contrast the distinction between hearing, active listening and passive listening. If you close your eyes you can hear what is going on around you (unless you have a hearing impediment) as well as inner sounds inside you. Even though we close our eyes we may well be interpreting what we are hearing from the sensation of the sounds – we will place meaning on the sounds through our listening. Even when we close our eyes we may listen by paying attention to what we hear. We could also be passive in simply not trying to grasp meaning from it or not really caring what we hear. Now with our eyes open we listen to somebody such as our presenter.

Listening actively is not just hearing what is being said but is a two-way process involving both sender and receiver skills. So, in the example of our presenter conveying her message about her work and promotion prospects, I as listener need to convey to her that I have received what she has tried to communicate. This is why active listening is a tough-minded process. We have to really work at it and if we are really listening it shows! The sender (presenter) is aware of the listener really listening.

Active listening also involves listening to the whole person, not just the words they may be using. Our culture emphasizes listening to what people *say*. We tend to listen at the level of our intellects. But active listening also includes listening to what a person's non-verbal messages are saying – *body* messages. In addition, as senders of messages we convey our *feelings*, that is the emotional content of our message. Lastly, we have another level which can be called our will, commitment or *spirit*. Let us take our example of the presenter talking about her potential promotion.

She is saying that she is considering going for the promotion because she is well-qualified for the post. Her body is sending out messages that convey something about her feelings toward the post, as is her tone of voice. Underlying these messages is another that is transmitted about her will or spirit to go for the promotion. If as listeners we merely went by what she said we would conclude that all she needs to do is to get on with the application form. However, by actively listening we are picking up more complex messages.

Contrast passive listening and the signals that are conveyed between the sender (presenter) and receiver (listener or set member). With passive listening the listener conveys, often non-verbally, that he is not really listening. Go through *SOLER* again and think of situations in which you have been on the receiving end of passive listening. Recall situations where you have given out the signals of passive listening to a person who wanted your attention!

Further aspects of effective listening

Apart from being passive towards the presenter there are other ways, which can overlap, that can impede the effectiveness of our listening.

Evaluative listening
When we listen evaluatively we may impose our own values upon the presenter's message. In our example of the presenter considering promotion, we may do any of the following whilst apparently listening:

think that she really hasn't a chance (or that it is a walkover);
feel jealous (why am I not going for it?);
feel dismissive (who would want the job anyway?);
make a judgement that she should not go for it.

The listener is judging what he is hearing whilst it is being transmitted instead of putting the thoughts to one side in order to hear what she is conveying. It is very difficult to put judgements aside entirely. It is important to recognize where they are coming from, however. Evaluations of the situation may be helpful at a later stage provided they enable her to move forward.

Inattentive listening
This occurs when as listener we are distracted by tiredness, our own emotions, or our difficulty with differences of culture, gender, race, sexual orientation or ability which 'get in the way' of listening.

Filtering listening according to the listener
Similar to the above, but more specifically the listener is filtering what the presenter is saying according to the listener's view of the world.

How shall I respond?
A listener preoccupied with this question (and it is understandable when we first become conscious of our responses) may stop listening and therefore attending to the presenter. However, really active listening will not require any preparation for the listener is already likely to be at one with the presenter.

Listening with sympathy
A common and human response, but sympathy can get in the way for the presenter. For example, if at a later meeting our presenter reports that she applied for the promotion but was 'pipped' to it by another candidate, we as listeners could offer our sympathy and model what we consider to be her feelings of sorrow and loss at not getting the promotion. If we collude in this or even foster it we, as listeners, are merely getting in the way of the presenter moving on to future action. We could be disabling in our effect. Being with her empathically is different, as we shall see below.

Listened to without interruption
Interrupting a person who is conveying her thoughts and feelings is a common trait in conversation arising from enthusiasm, boredom, having something to say ourselves, not being able to wait, emotion, or insensitivity toward the person speaking. In action learning sets one of the earliest reflections given by set members is, 'It is such a change being listened to without interruption'.

Given the time for each member of the set (25-40 minutes), a set member, when presenter, can use the early part of that time for herself. It is almost sacrosanct. It is for the other set members, as listeners, to take their cue from her before intervening.

One of the few exceptions to this is where the presenter has the need to take time to talk a matter through using most of her allotted time without receiving responses. The set adviser or other member of the set has to intervene to say that her allotted time has been used and that to continue will require agreement of the set members.

Listening with 'silence'
At times the presenter may pause or not want to express words. There may be a tendency for a set member to fill the silence or space with a question or a

response. There is, in fact, no silence – it is just that the presenter has stopped using words! That 'silence' can be precious for the presenter and for the set in being with the presenter without words. The time is the presenter's. It is space for her. If that space includes silence, it is to be respected.

Reflecting Back

Much of listening is communicating to the presenter non-verbally that we really are listening. However, this section is distinguished from the last in that the listener now responds to the presenter in order to clarify and confirm that what the listener has received is an accurate reflection of what the presenter conveyed.

Given that non-verbal reflection has been conveyed, the listener may respond with an 'um' or 'ahah' during the presenter's commentary. This may not be the case in a set situation where there are five to seven people. An 'um' response is more likely in a one-to-one situation. However, the set will still give that confirmatory nod or whatever to confirm the presenter.

Once the presenter has conveyed that she has concluded her story, any member of the set may respond. Indeed when used effectively it can mean that the presenter benefits from having a group of people attending to her with what may be called a 'collective wisdom'. One member may attune to the presenter more closely than others and follow it through with reflecting back what has been conveyed, along with clarifications.

Given that the set member will wish to reflect back what he thinks he has heard, he may wish to start with phrases like, 'What I think you said was . . .', or 'If I have understood you properly . . .'. The purpose here is to *accurately* reflect back to the presenter what the listener thought she said. Using the presenter's exact words in 'reverse' may be helpful, if the meaning is unclear. An inappropriate response would be to:

- give an interpretation of what was said rather than an accurate response;
- make and convey an assumption beyond what was said.

This description may appear simple, obvious or even banal as set out on this page. It is stated here because of our social tendency to assess and interpret and think what we are going to say even before the presenter has finished. It is an important process to disentangle so that we really are attending to the presenter and not imposing our own view of her reality.

The listener in responding should aim to do so in a way that is not pedantic or interrogative. The tone of voice is important. A tone which suggests criticism or a lack of caring or agreement is not helpful. The aim is to reflect back what is being said – the presenter's words and meaning; her emotions, her feelings; her will or spirit.

The reflecting back does not have to repeat the words our presenter used exactly. It is useful to paraphrase so that she can respond with say, 'Yes, that's it', or 'Not quite, I would put it like this', until there is assent between presenter and listener. Moreover, by paraphrasing the listener is also going beyond simply saying, 'I understand' when in fact he may not and he has not demonstrated to the presenter that he has and she does not really know he has understood. The use of the notorious phrase, 'I hear what you say' may also convey the same lack of real understanding between listener and presenter!

Active listening and reflecting or responding work in harness in the set. A set that is really working is concentrating in a way that conveys to the presenter that the set is with her. We will now move on to another aspect of interpersonal effectiveness between set members – disclosure.

Disclosure

A key condition for a set to be effective is that there is an atmosphere of trust amongst the set members and facilitator. By trust we mean that set members are willing to talk about themselves and disclose themselves in a way that is helpful to them. Having the rule of confidentiality is crucial to that sense of trust existing and being enhanced within the set.

In our interpersonal relations we vary the extent to which we are willing to convey what we are thinking and feeling. This variation is partly about trust. How far and how much we disclose may also be related to differences in culture, gender, class, race, sexual orientation, and disability. It is also about the nature of the relationship, for example:

- a loving partnership;
- a working relationship as
  - colleagues,
  - manager and managed;
- doctor and patient;
- woman to woman;
- man to man.

Any disclosure will be transmitted through messages between the sender and receiver (as we saw in the example, 'Losing the message') and subject to the same loss and potential misinterpretation. A person may also disclose intentionally or unintentionally.

The messages that convey the disclosure may be via:

- the body – face and parts of the body;
- the voice – how we talk;
- touch – physical contact with another;
- verbal – what we say;
- actions – what we do in contrast to what we say and how we say it.

In a set it is potentially useful for a set member to be open in their interactions with other set members. What does it mean to be more open in this context?

	Known to Self	Not known to Self
Known to Others	1 Open	2 Blind
Not Known to Others	3 Hidden	4 Unknown

Figure 9.1 *The Johari Window*

Johari Window

A very useful insight into how we may relate to people is the diagrammatic representation known as the Johari Awareness Model or Johari Window (a name derived from the authors' names) (Luft, 1984).

Interaction between two or more people depends on the extent of openness as well as the context in which it takes place. The square or window describes the possible forms of awareness of behaviour and feelings in a relationship. We will examine each quadrant in turn. The window represents a person we will call 'A'.

Quadrant 1 – the open quadrant, refers to the behaviour, feelings and motivations that 'I' (A) know about myself as well as others who see my behaviour. This is the window that A (and all of us) open to the world. It is the basis of most interaction that we willingly display.

Quadrant 2 – the blind quadrant, is that which refers to behaviour feelings and motivations that others see but which 'I' do not. This is the window A 'displays' to others without being aware that he is displaying it. In an interaction, person A displays himself as quadrant 1 – his public self. The person to whom he displays himself, person B, sees the public A but may also get an insight into A through quadrant 1 into quadrant 2 that A cannot 'see' or be aware of. For example, A may interact with B but not realize that in the interaction he inadvertently makes a sexist remark to B. Only if B points out the remark to A, will A be aware of it. How B conveys the message that A has made the remark and how A reacts to it will influence how A gets to know that particular blind spot.

Quadrant 3 – the hidden area, is that window which refers to behaviour, feelings and motivations which 'I' know about but which I am unwilling to convey to others. For example, A may be unwilling to disclose to C that he likes him, even though C may observe manifestations of that liking through A's window 2.

Quadrant 4 – the unknown area, is the part of ourselves that we do not know about, and is not known by others either. This window will contribute to our behaviour but neither we nor others normally see that part of ourselves. We may gain insights into it through our dreams when we sleep or even in the occasional day-dream, or we gain insight through therapy, and that is the place for it.

The total window is drawn to scale in Figures 9.1 and 9.2 for ease of representation. Luft (1984) suggests that quadrant 4 is much larger than displayed.

139

	Known to Self	Not Known to Self
Known to Others	1	2
Not Known to Others	3	4

Window a:unchanged   Window b:disclosing

Figure 9.2 *Disclosing*

Using the Johari Window we can see how disclosure works in an action learning set. Figure 9.2 represents a presenter, 4.

In window a in Figure 9.2 we have a starting point, say in a new set. In window b the presenter begins to disclose some of that which is hidden from the view of others from quadrant 3. With growing trust in interaction with B and others in a set, A will receive feedback about himself, window 2 which he

Window c – more open

Figure 9.3 *Disclosure and personal insight*

is unable to know without the insight of others. The result may be for A, a new presentation to the group represented by window c in Figure 9.3.

In interaction with other people and groups, A may return to the original window a in his interactions shown by the hatched line in Figure 9.3. A may well continue to use the insights into his behaviour from B and the set about quadrant 2 in his interactions with others outside that group. In other words, A has greater insight to himself (quadrant 2) and a range of choice of self-disclosure.

In relation to an action learning set it is possible to recognize how this could be happening for others in the set, even if not symmetrically. The effect is that disclosure may encourage disclosure across the set as well as an atmosphere of being able to give and receive feedback which may provide set members with insights about their quadrant 3.

Self-disclosure

The section on Johari has shown how, in an atmosphere of trust, in a set and with confidentiality we may offer to disclose ourselves to other set members. How do we go about saying what we wish to say?

'I' statements
In Chapter 6, we refer to how 'I' statements enable a person to *own* what he is saying as opposed to words like 'you', 'one', 'we', 'that', 'it'. When you wish to be clear about a message you are conveying, whether it is about your thoughts, feelings or actions, it is unambiguous when you start with the pronoun 'I'.

Telling it like a story
A useful distinction is between telling a message in the form of a story and telling it like history. We acknowledge the origins of the distinction in Egan (1973) and have adapted it to the set context.

'Story' is involvement; 'history' is non-involvement. History is a statement or message which is analytical, factual – it ticks off the facts of experience and even interpretation of these facts but leaves the person who is the revealer untouched, relatively unknown. The presentation can be long and even boring. The presenter is detached and uninvolved, taking no risks. The presenter treats herself as *object* rather than subject who is 'there and then'. Generalities may be disguised by the use of words like 'we', 'one' or 'it'. History does not reach or engage the listener. It is flat or boring because it is divorced from the person. It is not really disclosing the person.

'Story' on the other hand is not analytical. It is authentic self-disclosure – an attempt to reveal myself as a person and to reach the listener. Story involves emotion. Story is a signal of invitation – the presenter is opening the door to others in the set. It is a story if it is a description by the set member about themselves expressed, for example, as 'I felt really good about the way I challenged my manager on the way he addressed the staff as "girls", without making him feel inferior or blamed.'

Again, a story may start as a story but because the individual has worked through an issue it is no longer really an issue for her. One of us recalls taking time in a set to discuss what we considered to be important – it was about the use of time at work – and being challenged by another set member as the latter felt there was no real will or commitment about what was being described. The story had become history.

Another way of categorizing the difference is contrasting the words below:

Story	History
I	Them; it; people
Feeling; affect	Fact
Actual	Abstract
Real	Abstract; detached
Interesting	Boring; a turn-off

In other words, when we are expressing our feelings (the affective part of us) as well as the cognitive and conative, we are likely to be in story mode and disclosing something about us that has its basis in a real meaning that will make connections with the listeners.

Story is selective in detail – not necessarily complete in communicating fact, but complete in communicating self. The 'story' teller is taking a risk and knows it. By so doing the presenter requests support from set members. In a set, self-disclosure is a leap of trust – and demands dialogue 'here and now'. It is unusual not to be engaged when someone is telling their story. It is usually interesting. The presenter may have taken a risk, made herself vulnerable in the process but will not lose the set members' engagement. The set members will seldom be bored by such a story with sincere self-disclosure but they may be embarrassed.

The embarrassment can be a cultural bias against self-disclosure and the expression of emotion, seen in some contexts as a weakness at one extreme or exhibitionism at the other. Self-disclosure peaks in childhood and is seen as a passing phase that goes with oncoming maturity. In the fullness of time we become fully locked-in mature adults! However, as human beings we do not lose our emotions, they remain in us and can be a barrier to our development or can enhance that development. Self-disclosure is often associated with the psychiatrist's couch – we must be weak and in need of 'treatment'.

Fortunately, this model (a medical model) is becoming outmoded with our increasing understanding of ourselves as having subjective feelings which impinge on our everyday lives. For example, our presenter earlier in this chapter wanted to go for promotion. She was inhibited by a sense of lack of confidence which she was not really aware of. Getting feedback about how she was unaware of her demeanour in a supportive way enabled her to work on her confidence as a means of taking action. She may have known inside her that she was lacking confidence and trying to hide it. But to the set the demeanour showed (quadrant 2 in the Johari Window). The facts which she wished to hide were revealed in non-verbal clues.

Thus, telling it like a story is more likely to convey congruence between what we are saying and what we are feeling and what our thoughts really are. It is more likely to create bridges of understanding than taking no risks which can lead to misinterpretation.

Appropriateness of disclosure

Too much self-disclosure is embarrassing. Too little and we may find we do not relate to others and reduce our capacity to reflect upon ourselves in the set. Quadrant 3 in the Johari Window is hidden from our listeners. How far we disclose depends in part upon our values and the norms of the group. Some people value openness, others privacy. Self-disclosure reveals it. Over-disclosure occurs when the disclosure is inappropriate to the context.

The level of disclosure which is suitable to the context can be called 'appropriate self-disclosure'. 'Appropriate' is defined by:

● amount;
● depth;
● time;
● the target, ie, the person(s) talked to;
● the situation.

Our experience of action learning sets is that set members do engage in self-disclosure as the atmosphere of trust develops between members. We have seen earlier that the development of that trust depends on the set adhering to the ground rule of confidentiality. Knowing that what is said in the set will not be repeated by other set members outside the set is crucial. Action learning sets can provide the situation for a degree of self-disclosure that may not be available elsewhere.

Self-disclosure in a set provides a means of finding out about ourselves which we may not be aware of. Using Johari again, if I am more open towards other set members, I am conveying something of myself and conveying the *willingness* to do so. This willingness can encourage others to take the risk of disclosure about themselves. Moreover, it may give others the courage to convey to me something I may not be aware of in myself – in quadrant 2 of the Johari Window.

The facilitator can also model appropriate self-disclosure in the set even though she does not have set time for herself. Engaging in trauma, trivia and joy, for example, at the commencement of set meetings can help trust to develop (see Chapter 8).

Chapter 10

Additional Skills

The additional interpersonal skills we have identified include the expression of emotion and empathy. Using these additional skills creates a rapport between set members which enables the giving and receiving of feedback. In terms of the action part of action learning, the presenter can then focus and specify action with the support of set members.

Management of Emotion

With self-disclosure we can determine the extent to which we disclose ourselves. The disclosure by us is largely under our control and we have the right not to disclose. Emotions are not so easily controlled and may be released verbally and/or non-verbally. Yet we do seek to control the expression of our emotions even though we may feel them.

The purpose of this section is to suggest that a set can, with care and respect for each set member, enable the expression of emotions in a helpful way for each set member. A helpful way of expressing emotion is one that promotes congruent relationships, that is, appropriate emotional expression that underpins the relationships. Our emphasis in the previous chapter on telling our story as opposed to 'out there' history provided an example of an approach that encourages the expression of emotion.

In telling our story in a set when we disclose verbally we channel emotional expression through our words. However, emotions cannot always be channelled or controlled and may be expressed with other signs of emotion such as tears and laughter. Feelings about expressing emotions, particularly expressing negative emotions, will depend upon the values we hold as well as our self-awareness. However, one thing is paramount – the feeling itself is not at fault, it just exists. How we manage the expression of our emotions is partly dependent on the way we value our emotions, which in turn dictates a large part of our interpersonal style.

We manage our emotions from two points of view. We manage our own emotions and we manage our emotions in response to our relating with others. An example of the first would be if another person made me feel angry or hurt. An example of the second would be if another person made a hurtful remark and then realised it with some embarrassment. I might feel it was singularly inappropriate to have made the remark, but I do not have to compound his embarrassment with further comment.

In the last chapter we quoted Egan and Heron in asserting the tendency of British and American cultures not to have paid much attention, until recently, to the development of interpersonal skills. This is also true of the expression of emotion. Whilst there are intra-cultural differences, we tend to be socialized not to express our emotions except in well-defined contexts. Some emotions are more 'acceptable' than others. Laughter is more acceptable than crying. Showing pleasure is more acceptable than anger. Emotion can be seen as being irrational, not quite in control and therefore an unacceptable obstacle to social interaction.

In fact feelings and emotions are basic human characteristics. They are neither good nor bad, right nor wrong. How we handle our emotions is a learned style of behaviour. We may be socialized not to show some of our emotions, such as crying, or anger. As a consequence we may also not be able to handle it in ourselves or in others. For example, many men feel that to cry is to show weakness which is linked to a recognition that women are traditionally able to work with emotions requiring caring and nurturing. This has resulted, amongst other things, in a channelling of women into (and men away from) work that is supposed to require these qualities. Apart from the gender stereotyping which this has created, with its consequential discriminations, the bias has helped to diminish our attention to the expression of emotions.

Being socialized to discourage the expression of some of our emotions is useful. I may be angry with someone. That does not mean I can hit out physically or abuse them emotionally. However, some socialization may result in the inhibiting of the show of emotions so that we become fully 'locked-in' adults.

Jourard (1971) suggests that persons who are 'known' by others are healthier and happier than those who are not. The suppression of emotion in Jourard's view is a major component of stress in modern society. In our role as facilitators we have often heard a set member say that being able to give voice to and express their emotions has been a major breakthrough in tackling a major task in work or in life.

If a person does not express their emotions verbally there will be a tendency to 'leakage' – the non-verbal expression of the emotions. Both can of course be expressed together. Non-verbal expression will include tone of voice, gesture and body language. Verbally, emotions may also be expressed inadvertently when the words belie the intention, as in Freudian slips!

Positive or helpful expression of emotion

Emotion is present and normal and a part of all of us. How can we express or manage our emotions to good effect?

Emotions are OK

Emotions can get out of hand but that is about expression. Emotion in itself is a fact. We are living human beings for whom emotion is an integral part of ourselves. People who declare that they feel no emotion have just got the lid on tighter than the rest of us and will reveal 'leakages' in some way.

You may find that your interpersonal style is not characterized by the expression of feeling. Participation in an action learning set may give you the opportunity to explore your style in a safe environment.

Responsibility for emotion: owning it

We are each responsible for our emotions. If, say, someone lets me down I may feel angry. What do I do with my anger? I can respond with an accusation, 'You are making me feel angry', or 'I feel angry because . . .'.

With the latter I am taking responsibility for dealing with my own anger. This is important. If I make the former statement, the person to whom I am making it may feel accused, threatened and defensive.

Storing-up emotions

Saving or storing-up emotions is not helpful, for when they eventually emerge they may explode. It is better to express feelings as they arise even if they are negative. We may need a little time to identify what the emotion is and how we feel but that is different from putting the emotion into storage.

Assertiveness and expression of emotion

We have addressed assertiveness in Chapter 9. However, assertiveness has its place in emotional expression. If someone's behaviour is upsetting you then say so and why in terms of your own feelings, taking responsibility for your feelings as suggested above.

Knowing your own emotional states
Awareness of our emotional states enables us to express clearly in words what it is we are feeling and why. Set members may notice that they have difficulty expressing some emotions or express them indirectly.

Empathy

In action learning it is important for facilitators and set members to have and develop empathy. Empathy is one of the most valuable, if not the most valuable, relational skill we have. Empathy is used to enhance one-to-one relationships. We are using empathy here to add to the quality of set interactions.

By empathy we mean an ability to project oneself into another person's experience while remaining unconditionally oneself. Carl Rogers (1978) expresses it well; we have adapted the quote to action learning:

> Being empathic involves a choice on the part of the [facilitator] as to what she will pay attention to, namely the . . . world of the [set member] as that individual perceives it . . . it assists the [set member] in gaining a clearer understanding of, and hence a greater control over, her own world and her own behaviour.

In summary, empathy is an understanding of the world from the other's point of view, her feelings, experience and behaviour, and the communication of that understanding in full.

Egan (1976) built upon Rogers' ideas about empathy and developed a model of the skill which we adapt below.

Empathy is based on two pieces of information:

- what the speaker is feeling;
- the experience and/or behaviour which is the source of that feeling.

When these two pieces of information have been identified the next step is communication of the listener's awareness to the speaker. For example, I might say, 'John is really bugging me with the work overload'. The listener, if empathetic, will respond with something like, 'You feel upset because John is pressuring you'.

In starting to use empathy more explicitly the response is, 'You feel . . . because . . .', or 'You feel . . . when . . . because . . .', which can be a useful way to get into using the skill. Once familiar with the approach, using the skill will be less mechanical.

Egan (1976) describes a number of ways in which listeners have problems in effectively engaging in accurate empathy. We will refer his headings and adapt them to the action learning set context.

Let us take the following statement made by the presenter:

I see myself as so ordinary. I'm not the person for this promotion. I don't relate well to others. I'm ordinary.

Her statement can be followed by a number of less than appropriate responses by set members.

The cliché – responses like:

I hear what you say.
I understand.

These are of no help to the presenter. Such statements or clichés do not convey to the presenter that she is understood; they are more likely to convey to the presenter that she is *not* understood and that the set member is responding in an automatic and unauthentic manner.

The question – a response to our presenter's statement might be:

In what ways are you ordinary?

The question does not take account of the fact that our presenter has taken a risk in disclosing how she feels. The question does not convey empathic support about how and whether the set member is understanding her.

Interpretation – here the set member would respond by trying to adduce too early what is implied in the presenter's disclosure. An example might be:

This ordinary thing is the outward problem. I bet there's something else behind it that's upsetting you.

Inaccuracy – here the set member may just be plainly inaccurate with a response to the presenter like:

You're not very happy with the way the set is treating you

The presenter may be taken off-track or stop or hesitate because empathy, accurate empathy, has not happened and she may be blocked by what has been said. The set member may be listening to his own agenda about the presenter rather than attending to her.

Pretence – the presenter may have said the above at the end of a long and emotional description. The set member gets distracted by the length and possibly by the emotion but tries to convey that he understands, perhaps to avoid embarrassing the presenter by making it evident that she may not have been listened to accurately. However, such a pretence is not genuine and will only inhibit empathic support. It is quite appropriate for the set member to convey that he does not understand with phrases like:

I'm sorry, I was distracted for a moment. Could we start again please?
It seems to me that . . . but maybe I'm not getting it correctly.

The latter is tentative, suggesting to the presenter that maybe the set member has not understood her accurately. This leaves the presenter able to provide clarification and interaction with the set member until there is accurate understanding. It also indicates to the presenter that what she is saying is valued and important and encourages her to continue.

Responding too soon or too late – giving the presenter a chance to express herself gives the set member time to sort out feelings and content. However, spontaneity is valuable and 'interrupting' may be necessary if the presenter is beginning to ramble. Care needs to be taken here in order not to convey impatience.

Parroting – here the set member merely repeats back to the presenter what has been said. The set member needs to 'own' what has been said and then respond. This shows that the set member has got 'inside' the presenter in a way that conveys accurate empathy. Egan (1976) compares parroting with a tape recording where there is little mutuality or human contact. An effective response gets to the presenter in a way that parroting cannot.

Discrepancy – using language that is incongruent with the speaker's. Use similar language in response to that used by the speaker. This encourages rapport provided the language the responding set member uses is authentic to him. He then conveys that he is in tune with the presenter.

Longwindedness – rapport and understanding do depend on dialogue. If the presenter is conveying a story that is being attended to it may not be appropriate to intervene. Set meetings are more effective when set members realize that time has to be used with economy, that time is precious for each set member. A presenter conscious of her time, who nevertheless is able to convey her feelings with her content, will aim to be crisp with her description. Similarly, set members, when they intervene, will make their responses with precision to enable the dialogue to continue for the benefit of the presenter.

What empathy is not

Empathy is not:

- about giving advice;
- giving an evaluation;
- making a judgement;
- giving an interpretation;
- making a challenge;
- engaging the presenter in a re-orientation.

When a presenter shares a problem with the set, it is not necessary for set members to solve it for them, even though there might be the temptation! Your solution may not be appropriate anyway. Understanding of the presenter's problem or issue is much more useful – provided the set members communicate that understanding.

If set members are into solutions this could make for greater difficulty on the part of the presenter. Communication of understanding allows a presenter to move on to a discovery, in time, of her solutions and ways of handling them.

Empathy commits set members to the presenter and commits set members to stay with the presenter. That is a sign the presenter is valuable and worthwhile, to be respected.

The skill of empathy is rather rare in social interaction – few people experience it. When set members experience it they recognize the power of an understanding response that builds trust in a set. As facilitators of sets we have observed how set members acknowledge that they carry the skill discovered or enhanced in the set to other areas of their lives.

Giving and Receiving Feedback

The set may be able to give feedback to our presenter and she may wish to receive it. This is in contrast to the presenter self-disclosing. Here we are referring to the set members giving feedback that will be revelatory to the presenter. The Johari Window is again helpful here.

In Chapter 9 we saw how, via window 3 (that window which refers to behaviour, feelings and motivations which 'I' as presenter know about but which I am unwilling to convey to others) I am willing to disclose, when there are conditions of trust. The effect of the disclosure is shown by the arrows from

	Known to Self	Not Known to Self
Known to Others	1	2
Not Known to Others	3	4

Window a:unchanged

1 <<<<<<<	2
3	4

Window b:disclosure and feedback

Figure 10.1 *Disclosure and feedback*

quadrant 3 to quadrant 1. In window a we had the starting point, say in a new set. In window b the person began to disclose some of that which was hidden from the view of others from quadrant 3.

In giving feedback to the presenter other set members will enable our presenter to become aware of those behaviours, etc, of which she is unaware but which are evident to the set members. In Figure 10.1 the feedback is represented by the arrows from quadrant 2 to quadrant 1.

The result may be a new presentation to the group represented by window c in Figure 10.2. With growing trust in interaction with the others in the set, she will receive feedback about herself from window 2 which she is unable to know without the insight of others.

What are the necessary conditions for set members to give and for our presenter to receive appropriate feedback following and in addition to the skills of effective listening and empathy? The necessary conditions are a set of behaviours which can be summarized as a climate of support.

Climate of support

A climate of support will exist in the set when its members are being genuine, ie spontaneous, open, role-free and not defensive. In addition, set members will offer respect to the presenter by giving their attention in a non-

Window c – more open

Figure 10.2 *Effect of disclosure and feedback*

judgemental way and demonstrating a willingness to work with and for the presenter.

By 'genuine' we mean that the set members are being themselves rather than playing a role. An example of a set member in role could be where the member is, say, a manager at work, and he carries that role into the set, with the result that the presenter is unable to share her feelings for fear of a managerial response.

By 'defensive' we mean where any member of the set, including a presenter, is unable to accept feedback from colleagues, thereby isolating herself from the set. An example would be where the presenter exceeds her time and when this is called to her attention blames the set members rather than taking responsibility herself.

By 'non-judgemental respect' we mean behaviour which values the individual presenter as a unique person in her own right, suspends value judgements about her or her issue, accepting that she can determine her own course of action. It is useful to note here that these conditions coincide with the prerequisites for empathy addressed in the previous section.

If there is no trust and support in the set, feedback, however accurate, may not be heard, that is, it may not be received. In terms of the Johari Window for our presenter, quadrant 2 is inaccessible to her. Assuming a climate of support exists in the set, the giving and receiving of feedback is likely to occur.

How to give effective feedback

We can now consider how set members can give effective feedback. It may be useful to note that term 'feedback' comes from an engineering and systems model. The feedback loop is designed to inform the system about change. Positive feedback signals change, negative feedback no change.

Clarity
Be clear about what you want to say in advance. Think about what it is you wish to say and the way in which you want to say it.

Emphasize the positive
Our culture tends to emphasize the negative with a focus more on weaknesses than strengths. Most people need encouragement, to be told when they are doing something well, despite being in circumstances of difficulty. This does not mean being collusive with the presenter's circumstances. For example, a presenter was preparing to leave a full-time job to become independent. She conveyed that she feared being unemployed. A set member intervened to ask her whether she would be unemployed or self-employed. It was an insight offered that enabled the presenter to be positive about herself. The feedback was significant to her own self-image as well as being realistic.

Be specific
Avoid general comments which are not very useful to the presenter. If superlatives like, 'That was brilliant . . .', or 'That must have been hard . . .', are used, follow them up with specific statements about what was brilliant or hard, and why. We will consider statement-specific language later in the chapter.

Select the priorities
It is the presenter's time. Convey the feedback in precise form that gets to the core or essence for the presenter. One set member may convey broadly what another set member may have said. There is usually little virtue in repeating the same.

A set member may have an idea that takes the presenter forward; however, another set member intervenes with something else which the presenter picks up and 'runs with'. A memorable example of this was the occasion when a set member later in a review session said he had been itching to convey an idea but it was, 'An idea whose time was gone'. The set member lets it drop if he considers it of no use to the presenter. It is not to the presenter's benefit if the set member simply conveys the idea to get it off his chest.

Focus on behaviour rather than the person

The presenter may have disclosed her feelings about her work and what she felt has happened to her. It is more effective if set members respond with feedback that adduces specific behaviours she engaged in rather than broad statements like, 'You were ineffective with your manager'.

Refer to behaviour that can be changed

It is no use giving a presenter feedback on something in which they may have no choice, for example responding to a presenter who is committed to a job yet currently in a difficult predicament with a statement like 'Well, you could always leave'.

Be descriptive rather than evaluative

Rather than merely saying that something was good, be specific about what it was the presenter said that was good.

Own the feedback

Here we emphasize again the use of 'I' statements in preference to using words like 'one', 'you' or 'they', which convey a specious universality of agreed opinion. Using 'I' at the beginning of the feedback is important in showing that we are taking responsibility for that feedback.

What the feedback says about the set member

Feedback is likely to say as much about the set member giving it as the receiving presenter. The feedback will say a good deal about the set member's values and what he focuses on with others. Therefore the set member can learn about himself if he listens to the feedback he gives.

Receiving feedback

Listen to the feedback before responding

There is a tendency to respond to feedback immediately. Feedback can be uncomfortable to hear but we may be poorer without it. Feedback may give us insights which otherwise we may miss. The conditions in a set of genuineness and respect will underline the feedback given.

Be clear about what is being said

The presenter receiving feedback can check that what she has heard is accurate before responding to it. She may also wish to hear other set members and their feedback before responding.

Window c – more open

Figure 10.3 *Effect of disclosure and feedback for the set*

Decide what to do as a result of the feedback

When our presenter receives feedback she can assess its value, the consequences of using it or ignoring it and then decide what she will do as a result of it. In the final analysis it is the presenter's choice what to do with the feedback.

In summary, the better presenters are at receiving feedback the more they encourage set members to give feedback. If a presenter demonstrates that she can receive it, she will help others to receive it. We can view the Johari Window c again in Figure 10.3 as a window for the whole set. As disclosure (quadrant 3) occurs and feedback becomes culturally acceptable in the set (quadrant 2 becomes more available for each set member) so the set attains a larger quadrant 1. From this more effective work can be done by each set member.

'Shoulds' and 'Oughts'

When set members are conveying their story, they often use words like 'should', 'shouldn't', 'ought', 'oughtn't', 'must' and 'mustn't'.

Let us convey an example. A set member has decided to bring the progressing of her postgraduate research as her task for the set. It is a doctoral thesis in its sixth year. She is burdened by the whole thing and wants it out of the way (as does her thesis supervisor) by completing it in the next year. Much has been done on it but the thesis has been in a state of lapse for a year. Life has taken new turns and the PhD is no longer top of the agenda.

She has been making superficial progress for the last month or so. As presenter, she is talking about her progress:

> I have had another meeting with my supervisor. I didn't feel too good about the few pages I've done since I last saw her. She suggested I move to another chapter instead of being stuck with the current chapter. She asked me when I wanted to go for completion (of the thesis). I said that I should finish it by October next. . . .

There followed some clarification questions around the detail of the chapters she was moving from and to. After a few moments a set member asked her (in great contrast to the detail of the previous questions):

> Are you doing this PhD because you ought to or because you want to?

The set member said it in a caring manner and toward the end of the presenter's time. She paused and did not answer. After some time she said that she needed to think that one through between now and the next set. The set left it at that. At the next meeting she said the question had stopped her in her tracks because she had not clarified that distinction even at the commencement of the research six years ago when she had finished her first degree.:

> The question faced me centrally about my commitment to the research. If it was a should or ought then there was a kind of rule that I was adhering to that did not necessarily have anything to do with me. If I want to do it, that is because of something in me that drives me – no one else. I have cleared in my mind that I want to do it, I want to complete it and have said that to my supervisor. Moreover, I have talked about it with my partner and at work and they acknowledge the pressure I will have for a few months and are with me. It helped enormously, once I was clear what I wanted, to talk through the implications with them.

We do not know, as she informs us, whether she started the research wanting to do it or because it had been an ought. She may have felt obliged to do to it because it was:

- the 'done thing';
- some well-meaning 'others' wanting her to do it – colleague graduates, lecturers, parents, friends;
- it would be a good career marker.

However, she may also have started it because she actually wanted to (through interest in the discipline, area, etc), but it may have become an implicit 'ought' during the period.

She could well have decided between the set meetings that the thesis was an ought and given up or proceeded with the ought to a conclusion. The significance was that she recognized the reasons: what she actually wanted; what she was doing; and the desire to complete it – which enabled her to move the pace and progress to completion in the time agreed with her supervisor!

This story conveys the effect of these key words we often use. We may have oughts but we do have the choice as to whether we do them or not. The cost of not doing an ought may be high for the person – but that is their choice; the set has merely enabled her to make a clearer choice.

The other words we tend to use are 'must' or 'mustn't' or 'can't'. A set member may say, 'I must get this report in by the first'. This can be followed by the thought, 'Can you imagine what would happen if you didn't?' Similarly, 'I can't have three weeks for a holiday this year', followed by, 'I wonder what would happen if you did?'

These questions may be easier to ask ourselves. Asking them of other set members will require care. The framing of the question may be construed as implying that the set member should throw caution to the wind and be obtuse. Remember, it is the set member's life and responsibilities that are being addressed.

Generalizations

Another way in which we construct the world is to make generalizations that we apply to ourselves.

A presenter may tie himself up with statements like, 'I can't stand the managers at my company. They are all a bunch of autocrats'. He may have actually experienced three managers who are like that. However, he is making a generalization about all the other managers in the organization. Making that generalization may influence how he relates to other managers. No matter how approachable the other managers he comes across he is still influenced by that main thought.

A set member may have been given notice of termination of employment and is faced with the prospect of unemployment. Self-perception may be reinforced by statements like, 'No one will want to employ me. I am too old (too loud, too pushy, too young, a woman, black, past my sell-by date)'.

Behind this statement (or its variations) may well be a wider macro-economic condition of widespread unemployment and organizations that are ageist, sexist or racist. Let that be acknowledged. But our set member is adding to the difficulty by excluding him- or herself by virtue of the generalization.

In a set it is useful for set members and the set adviser to keep an ear out for generalization, so that the presenter can be supported in examining a phrase that they may well have applied to himself in a way that acts as a block. In relation to the employment phrase above, a set member may say, simply, 'No one?', or 'No one will want to employ you?', with voice tone raised toward the end of the question, enabling the presenter to examine the meaning he has applied to himself.

Watch out for words like 'all', 'never', 'every(one)', 'always' and 'they', too. Putting a question mark after each of these words can help to expose them for what they may be – generalizations. Rarely are generalizations true *all* the time. By generalizing we stop ourselves from looking for exceptions to the rule. We also probably engage in more excluding of ourselves where we are involved. Recognize these words for what they often, but not always, are: limiting forms of behaviour.

Specifying Actions

An important part of the action learning process is that point when a participant has reviewed their progress on an issue and after consideration and reflection on where he is now, has to decide upon the next step to take after the meeting and before the next meeting.

This usually follows a question from another set member or the facilitator like, 'So John, what's your next step?', or 'Where do you go from here, Mary?'. The action or actions the set member takes are important in enabling John or Mary to make things happen in relation to their issues rather than just reflecting upon the issues. Action learning is about providing the place for reflection on a set member's experience but also to learn from that reflection and move forward from what has been learned in order to make effective the action in future experience.

Before the presenter concludes his time, it is usual to determine the action(s) he wishes to take that he will aim to fulfil by the next set meeting. The words set presenter use to specify their intended actions are crucial. The words and sentences should be active and specific like:

- I will do X by the next set meeting.
- I will acquire Y by 3 November.
- I will practise giving myself one hour a week for planning the week ahead.
- I will write and complete chapter 10 by 4 July.
- I will tell J that I will make the deadline for the report on the 16th of this month rather than the 10th.

The presenter making these intentions could have questions as follow-ups to make even more specific and concrete his actions. Take the last example. Questions that make the action more specific and concrete for the set member could be:

When will you tell J? and/or
When is it most appropriate for you to tell J?
Where will you tell J?
How will you tell J your change of deadline?

and possibly, depending on the issues/relationship between the presenter and J:

What if J declines to accept the revised date?

The benefit to the presenter of these further questions is that they enable him to clarify and break down the detailed actions that may lie within a broadly stated action. In the example above, our presenter can think about the implications of 'telling J' and as a result be more prepared to ensure that the intention of a new deadline of the 16th of the month is attained.

Another benefit is that we all have different ways of seeing the world. Attaining a specific deadline in this example may appear, superficially, to be the same thing or have the same meaning to all in the set. Only by asking some of the more detailed questions will the set begin to approximate similar views and meanings of the set member's intention (reality). If the set had stopped at the first statement about the date of the revised deadline members may have made assumptions about the when, where, how and what ifs, which if ignored may have affected the success of our presenter in attaining his revised deadline.

These further questions may not always be necessary and set time may limit putting them. But supposing in the example above the presenter was informing his line manager of the revised deadline. Further questioning may well help the set member ensure the most appropriate context to secure his aim. Without these questions we may have assumed that 'telling' was sufficient! Placing the word 'telling' on its own conveys how unspecific the word can be.

Contrast the initial reasonably specific statements above with the following:

- I will look at . . .
- I will address the issue of . . .
- I will consider . . .
- I will bear in mind . . .
- I will think about . . .
- I will discuss . . .

The latter statements are loose in their application to specific and concrete actions to be taken by the set member. They may be considered concrete by the set member but we do not really know. The phrases can all be followed up with the question:

How will you consider . . .? or
What specifically will you do . . .?
What specifically are you trying to achieve?

These questions (or variations on them) will provide him with a closer focus on what he can actually do.

Remember that the set process is not an interrogation or a cross-examination. Use questioning with the set member's interests at the heart of the process, so that questions like those in the last paragraph might be softened and given a tentative flavour by:

I'm wondering what, specifically, you mean by . . . or
What, perhaps, could you do specifically to . . .?

Occasionally the reflection or story is so significant for the presenter that no action is required. He just needs to let the experience in his time in the set settle. For example, one of us was pursuing a project, preparing a postgraduate course for validation. Each set meeting would be used to consider problems to move the course toward successful validation. On one occasion, however, the feelings that I came to the set with had overwhelmed the task that I had brought to the set. Whilst I did not intend to, I found myself trusting the group to be able to disclose my feelings about a very important personal event that was overriding the task. I just let the feelings emerge and talked about what was happening at that point in my life. My colleagues in the set listened, empathized and gently pointed out the proximity of my time at the set meeting coming to an end and would I like an extension with the agreement of the set? I thanked them and declined. No action questions were posed. The set realized, as I had, that it was sufficient for me to have shared my feelings. After the set meeting I felt much lighter and regenerated and incidentally made ample progress on the task.

We would not wish to be rigid in asserting that every set member has to come up with action(s) every set meeting following their presentation and interaction with the set. Further, a presenter may on occasion tell her story, and the telling has an impact so powerful for her that her learning resides in the reflection. No specific action is required. We could say that the action is that no specific action is required!

PART III

THE USES OF ACTION LEARNING

Chapter 11

Key Issues for Management Development

The purpose of this chapter is to develop key issues which underpin action learning as a relevant contribution to management development. We consider what organizations need to encourage in their staff to cope in conditions of uncertainty; the nature of training and development and the significance of the latter; what we mean by management development; and the levels at which organizations may embrace development.

We use the term management development in three ways: to the development of the individual manager in the organization; the systems of management development to meet particular individual manager needs; and as a contribution to the development of the organization as a whole.

The Changing Nature of Organizational Life

The justification for using action learning as a significant process contributing to manager and organizational development is based upon the effectiveness of action learning as a developmental process. Action learning processes for individuals, groups of staff and organizations can contribute to their ability to work actively with uncertainty and continuous change.

The era of relatively predictable futures, linear development, rationality, formality, tight hierarchies and specialization is in decline, yet many organizations and the people who work within them still live the culture and expectations of that era. Many writers, organizational theorists and practitioners have witnessed the atrophy of organizations in this mode and the need for different mindsets or ways of seeing the world (Handy, 1991; Kanter, 1981, 1989; Morgan, 1986, 1988; Peters, 1987).

Peters (1987) describes how we live in a world of 'generic uncertainty' where technology, competition and ever-changing tastes require: market niche orientation with shorter production runs; international outlook and action; flatter, more responsive and stand-alone organizations within large organizations; a concern with quality and a closer customer orientation; participation adding value through people.

Handy (1991), in appraising the nature of change, conveys neatly what is happening: 'that the changes are different this time: they are discontinuous and not part of a pattern . . .' By the changes being different this time, Handy means that in the recent past, change did occur for us but it could be largely prefigured, like the anticipated stages of a professional career, where there might be some unanticipated events but they were usually 'more of the same only better' (ibid), incremental in nature. Embracing discontinuity in the nature of work would be where an individual can contemplate that 'work' may well take different forms, be on the periphery of an organization(s), change radically in its nature over the years, and live with the anticipation that it is likely to be very different in the future from what it is now.

The problem with change that is framed round more of the same and mere incremental change is that our thinking and learning is caught within that frame:

> In a world of incremental change it is sensible to ape your elders in order to take over where they leave off, in both knowledge and responsibility. But under conditions of discontinuity it is no longer obvious that their ways should continue to be your ways; we may need new rules for new ball games and will have to discover them for ourselves. Learning then becomes the voyage of exploration, questing and experimenting. . . . (ibid)

One of the questions therefore is how organizations respond to create that reflective learning environment conducive to their maintenance, sustainability, survival, growth or transformation.[1]

---

[1] Even here we are aware of not trying to forecast the future. We hesitate to use the term 'growth', the most recent positive word associated with firms, particularly in the private sector, without the other terms attached, like 'sustainability' which may also have greater plausibility for some organizational forms.

Such reflective and questioning learning is potentially rebellious and an affront to those who control the way 'things are done around here'. But that is a reflection of the learning that is necessary – questioning that which is given. 'This is the way things are done around here' without questioning can lead to catastrophe. Did there have to be a catastrophe like that at King's Cross for smoking to be banned entirely from London's underground rail system? Handy uses the example of the *Titanic* for another catastrophe having to happen before lifeboats were provided for all passengers. Whilst these may be extreme examples, more likely scenarios are a gradual demise of organizations whose purposes are fixed in the past and remain so.

For organizations to actively counter a fixed view means creating a working environment where its members individually and collectively can get into that learning, questioning mode to cope actively with discontinuous change. For Handy (1991), a significant arena will be in our work: 'that it is the changes in the way our *work* is organised which will make the biggest differences to the way we all *live*' (emphasis in original).

Thus the only consistent feature of organizational life is change. A key for us is how people respond to the effect of this truism. Given the lack of choice about change, our personal experience of working in organizations is that people are trying to cope with the change that is happening around the organization and with the consequences within the organization. The phrase 'trying to cope' is used intentionally. Many are aware of the rapidity of change. However a person may be aware of the change but be passive to or even a victim of that change. Or it can mean that a person is actively aware of the process of change as an agent and is actively working with the flow of that change for their benefit and for organizational benefits. This book is a contribution to enabling people more actively to live and work with the flow of discontinuous change.

Morgan (1988) is concerned with the demands that these changes will make on the competences required of managers and staff in the years ahead. In the light of the debate and activity around the idea of competences in the UK, we would concur with Morgan's definition:

Now more than ever, organisations and their members face the dual problem of how to do it right *and* how to do it well. In the process, the whole concept of competence is changing. Whereas, in the past managerial competence went hand in hand with the possession of specific skills and abilities, it now seems to involve much more. Increasingly, it rests in the development of attitudes, values, and 'mindsets' that allow managers to confront, understand, and deal with a wide range of forces within and outside their organisations, as well as in the development of operational skills. (Emphasis in original)

Whilst managers and staff still require specific skills and abilities they also require to enrich and sustain their mindsets to assess the relevance and implications of what they are doing so that they 'become competent at being competent' (ibid). It is in this framework that we can relate management development to action learning.

Managers: Training and Development

In the remainder of this chapter we define our view of who managers are; distinguish training and development; distinguish manager development from management development; and define management development in two ways: as the systems required for manager development to occur and as organizational learning.

Managers: who is included?

We take a very broad definition of managers as people who *take* responsibility for their lives and work. In this sense 'everyone a manager' enables all staff to think and act managerially (Boydell *et al*, 1991). This also means that an organization can consider all staff in terms of their developmental needs.

We acknowledge that a narrower definition of manager can be made. Burgoyne (1988) when writing of the manager's development refers to managing that 'shapes' both itself and non-managerial work, which is 'what makes it [managing] different from other forms of work and what makes management development different from other areas of human resource development'. Thus some managers are also shapers.

We will maintain the two notions of 'everyone a manager' and some managers having an additional responsibility for the management of others.

Core activities?

Handy (1991) likens a person's work to the idea of a doughnut or, more appropriately, a bagel. The inner circle of the bagel represents the core of the person's or manager's work. For many in the past that represented the whole of their work. Beyond that was a clear boundary where someone else had a responsibility. That inner circle still exists for many but there is an outer circle of the bagel which is now a much more fluid, discretionary part of work which overlaps with the outer circle of others.

This trend is reflected in the traditional tendency for firm and clear divisions of responsibility for processes and tasks being replaced by an enhancement of many work roles in organizations, given technological advances and a move towards more integrated organizational design. The traditional mechanistic division often resulted in attitudes such as, 'Well, that's outside my brief, I can't help you', which is being replaced by 'How can we work through this task given our different starting points?'. Instead of emphasizing points of demarcation, we move to 'Where and how can we work on this problem?' This distinction highlights the contrast between the person who seeks to delimit her responsibility and the person who starts from a point of wishing to take responsibility for work for themselves, with colleagues and in the organization. This is not to be interpreted as a recipe for exploitation, more one of enabling individuals to meet their needs with others.

Thus managers are people who take responsibility for their lives and work, some shaping the work of others as well, who are increasingly working with others to achieve organizational and mutual ends. How do managers achieve these ends effectively through their training and development?

Training and development

A distinction may be made between training and development. There is an overlap between the two. We emphasize the distinction because the words are often used loosely and interchangeably. Action learning is primarily a developmental activity.

Training
By training we envisage an emphasis upon the acquisition by individuals of specific, identifiable skills, adding to or extending existing skills. In training the individual is likely to have training done for them or to them, typically where the person providing the training is 'up-front'. Alternatively, the individual may have some self-help manual to support them. Thus training is about:

> the transfer of knowledge or skills from one who knows or can to the one who does not or cannot . . . the trainer is the expert, the knowledgeable or skilled one; the learner is ignorant or unskilled (Boydell *et al*, 1991).

Training is a prerequisite to doing many tasks and jobs efficiently, like driving a car or operating a computer, using a lathe or learning a new language. All organizations require a whole range of skills to be able to make the product and provide a service. They are vital and necessary but not a sufficient condition for an individual or an organization to cope with let alone thrive on change – the one single unending imperative.

Revans (1983) locates the place of training with his famous equation:

$$L = P + Q$$

where L is learning, P is the acquisition of programmed knowledge and Q is questioning insight. Training quite rightly represents P, a prerequisite of learning but only half the picture. P is, in Revans' phrase, 'the stuff of traditional instruction'.

Training is an essential part of many jobs and professions. Training is about transferring knowledge and/or skills to people coming into or moving within the labour market into organizations. These skills and understandings are about the maintenance of the organization. For example, in the social services or transport there are skills intrinsic to the running of those services, without which they would not be able to operate. However, these services do not operate in a stable, unchanging environment. The people who work in them and the organizations they work for have to adapt and anticipate the changes that are going to happen to survive, meet client/customer needs and continue to be effective. Boydell *et al* (1991) express it thus:

> Now we need people who can flex and adapt quickly, who develop complex and *personal* repertoires of skills and responses which enable them to get by and survive and prosper. People who can forget skills as quickly as they can learn them are more likely to be valued in a world where organisations are formed and dissolved in half a generation rather than over generations of seemingly predictable progression (emphasis in original).

We would add that Revans' Q places the individual in a different stance to the person who is being trained to a level of skill and knowledge required to undertake a task or job. Having a questioning insight places the emphasis on the individual as a learner, taking responsibility for their learning process – learning about how to learn (additional to what is being learned), as opposed to it being the primary responsibility of the trainer, instructor or coach. It is the ability to work Q with facility that develops in managers that capacity to 'flex and adapt quickly'. This requires attention to the development of managers in addition to necessary training.

Development
Development is more complex and may incorporate some training. A person may need to train to touch-type in order to use a word processor effectively for creative work – a developmental activity – as well as learning and the principle of taking responsibility as set out above. So what else does development mean? Boydell *et al* (op cit) define development as, 'working with individuals or organisations to enable them to cross a threshold which has qualitative significance to them and their life'.

Development is more open-ended and holistic. By holistic we mean that the person may be engaging in a multi-faceted task where the effect of the whole is greater than and more significant than the sum of the parts. For example, a personnel manager in a negotiation role will bring a whole variety of interpersonal skills and understanding into the role which, combined, will contribute to the overall negotiation context. Moving into that role can involve some initial training on, say, negotiation and bargaining, but the whole of that role will involve development on the part of the personnel manager that is wider than those skills learned and applied in isolation.

Development can take place naturally in the course of maturity and experience. However, we are using the term in a conscious sense of people thinking about, actively reflecting on and learning from their experience. There is a much greater sense of active responsibility on the part of the individual to take control of their development. Development is also more open-ended than the more specific ends associated with training. In development there are no 'right answers', though there will be the exercise of judgement, wisdom and raising of more questions. This does not mean developing people to be less decisive or immobile either! Action without reflection may result in disaster. Reflection without action may be very useful provided the individual is aware of the repercussions of that stance. We are asserting that action with reflection will combine in development of the individual and, when with others, with their development as well. It is critical that the manager is able to legitimately reflect and think as an integral part of their development.

There are other characteristics of development for individuals that can be identified. Boydell *et al* use a universal example by tracing a child's development of mobility. A child moves through phases from being static, to rolling, crawling, walking and running. We will utilize these characteristics and draw upon the experience of becoming aware of and working with sexism as an example of personal development which had work and life implications for one of us. The characteristics of development are set out in numbered stages for analytical purposes. Obviously they are not so neat or necessarily sequential in reality.

1. The notion that development is both continuous and discontinuous process

> I became aware intellectually of the idea of sexism in my 30s. I incorporated the value of being non-sexist into my beliefs and vocabulary – what I espouse and what I say. There is discontinuity from the earlier stage when I was not aware of the idea and behaviour associated with sexism.

This phase ended in crisis . . .

2. marked by discrepancy and incongruence which is experienced as shock, surprise and causes the disintegration of the previous phase of functioning and creates the condition for the discontinuous 'step-jump' to a new phase.

> The new shock or incident that made for discontinuity was a behaviour by me that was pointed out as very sexist (it was) which I had not been conscious of at the time I said it, yet was in contradiction with my espoused values. In other words my espoused values were in conflict with my values in use, or what I *believed* differed from my *practice*!

In Handy's (1991) phrase it was the time when 'continuity ran out' and I had nothing to fall back on faced with the fact of my incongruity of behaviour. The shock, recognition and dramatic incongruity leads to a reframing and transforms my values of the earlier phase in 1.

3. There has to be a 'readiness' for that development to happen; we cannot be forced, only encouraged.

> I now realized that in the arena of dealing with my sexism what I do is even more important than what I believe. Despite the realization of my continued sexism in my behaviour I am ready to move on rather than not move on. If I am not ready I cannot move on.

4. Development takes place over time and over the life cycle. Some development occurs as a result of crucial phases in the life cycle, eg puberty, starting work or a family, retirement. Development is about the whole person, group or organization.

> In the example of my attendance to my sexism I am struck by how my behaviour had repercussions upon all my life, not just work. I begin to integrate the values, behaviour and actions into my life and work.

5. Development is progressive, one way, towards growth, though occasionally we may regress, say, in times of crisis but we cannot revert to a position we have left forever. Normally we aspire to greater understanding, more effective behaviour, etc, but occasionally things happen that remind us of having been here before . . .

> Like times when I still echo some old sexist traits but they are not usually as grotesque as the one that created the earlier crisis.
> Even if I 'reverted' to my old sexist ways and behaviours, I would be doing so knowing where I had been more recently and would have to live with that.

6. Development is not easy or inevitable. We may get stuck, cautious, very comfortable and defensive on occasion. In times of acute personal (and organizational) difficulty, survival and maintaining ourselves may be more important than developing. Wanting to develop may be desired but might just not 'happen'.

> Whilst I made for integration of anti-sexism in my personal relationships, there have been and are times when I have been hesitant and defensive about that integration.

7. Development is an upward spiral in which we may still meet old problems but at a more subtle level.

> Now working with equal opportunities in a developmental way with individuals and organizations, problems still emerge for me but at a different level. An example for me is, when is it appropriate to challenge a colleague engaged in an equal opportunities development programme?

We can build on this personal example of development by relating it to manager and organizational development in respect to the implementation of an organization's equal opportunities policies. For an organization to effectively implement such policies each manager may go through a complex process similar to that outlined above. Our view is that it is not simply a matter of personal change that a manager may experience (even though that is a necessary condition). A manager and the organization will, if the implementation and integration are to be successful, need to work with changes in practice and working relationships. For example managers will wish to model good practice in those relationships: be it, do it. They will need to be able to manage the changed expectations of staff and possible conflict arising among staff. The organization will wish to model good practice by removing institutional discrimination and creating the conditions for good practice.

A recent example where one of us was engaged in the implementation of an equal opportunities policy in a public sector organization is useful here. All managers undertook internal workshop development. On completion of the workshops many of the managers recognized their own personal change and development. However, it would not be sufficient just to leave the personal development there. That alone would not bring about the necessary changes in working practices for effective implementation of the policy. Incorporated into the workshops and integrated into their work and that of the organization and its collective action were tasks, actions and processes that were to be built in to integrate the policy into the life of the organization and its members. Actions in relation to recruitment, selection and retention of staff as well as attention to the equalities issues relating to the quality of the service also had to be built in.

In summary, development is a complex activity and complementary to training. I may need to learn and acquire a new and specific IT skill. The organization may need to ensure that its staff get word processor and spreadsheet skills to keep up with IT developments. But, as we have seen above, development is not something that can be just acquired, added on. Development is in the hands of every individual and collections of individuals as groups or organizations. As Boydell *et al* describe it, 'The impulse, ownership and evaluation belong to the developing being' (ibid).

The conditions for the effective development of each individual manager need to be created. How that development is encouraged, nurtured and enhanced is critical to the development of the organization.

Manager Development and Management Development

We make a distinction between manager development and management development.

The manager's development

By the manager's development we mean development that is consciously undertaken by the individual manager for her purposes. Her development is about 'the process of change, learning and development that affects how the person shapes and performs [their] tasks, roles and activities' (Burgoyne, 1988). The capacity of the organization to learn, survive and work with an ever-changing environment will depend upon the energy deriving from its staff and managers. That energy amongst managers will in turn partly depend upon the kind of developmental activities they engage in. The key questions that ensure energy is creatively harnessed will be:

- Does the developmental activity really *engage* the manager in her personal development in work and life?
- Does she have *ownership* of her development?
- Is the organization prepared to let the development of the managers happen in a way which engages their *energies* and *empowers* them?

Once these questions are recognized the organization supporting the manager's development can legitimately ask the following:

- What are the *benefits* to the organization of her development?
- What *value is added* to the organization by that development?

Note that there is a balance to be achieved here between meeting the legitimate needs of the individual and the consequential benefits for the organization.

Management development

By management development we refer to two distinct aspects:

[a] The totality of development that is undertaken by the organization for its staff – systems, structures and processes. We will call this the 'systems' of management development. These would include, for example, appraisal systems, career planning, planned and formal development on and off the job. Coaching, mentoring and action learning would be considered forms of planned development on the job.

[b] The effect of [a] on the organization as a whole – the synergy and learning that is achieved by the organization. We will call this the 'organizational learning'. This is now characterized by the term the 'learning company'.

Manager development and both aspects of management development interrelate. The systems of management development that are initiated by the organization will influence the quality of manager development – [a]. The quality of manager development that is achieved will influence the extent and

Figure 11.1 *The totality of development*

quality of organizational learning that is achieved – [b]. This can be represented in Figure 11.1 where IMD is individual manager development and [a] and [b] are as defined above.

To use an old metaphor – the engine of development is in the people in the organization in terms of the energy they bring to their development. The systems of management development are the starter motor for individual development which in turn leads to group and organizational development. In effective individual manager development, rest the bases for that management development of the organization which is about the organization's learning and its capacity for learning.

Burgoyne (1988) writes of his concern for the emphasis:

> to focus too much on the individual manager [IMD] and the organisational systems [a] dedicated to his or occasionally her development, and too little on management development for the organisation as a whole.[b]

We have inserted in parentheses our notation from Figure 11.1 to link our distinctions about management development with Burgoyne's comment.

Burgoyne has provided a valuable model in which to place the contribution of the systems for development [a] and the development of the organization as a whole [b]. Burgoyne considers there are six levels of maturity of organizational management development defined as 'the management of managerial careers in an organisational context', [a] above.

We shall briefly review the levels of maturity and then in the next chapter consider how action learning can contribute to manager development and organizational management development [b].

Levels of management development policy
(adopted from Burgoyne, 1988)

Level 1

At this level there is no systematic or deliberate management development. What takes place is 'natural' management development where development for individuals happens as a result of people living and working. Development is intuitive, there is no conscious planning of development. This level is most likely to occur and be effective where the organization is new, relatively small and at an entrepreneurial stage.

Level 2

Here the organization responds to development through isolated and piecemeal activities resulting from imperatives facing the organization such as a felt or emulated need to engage in staff appraisal, quality or performance measurement.

Level 3

At this level there is a coherent link between the development needs of individuals identified at appraisals with career plans designed to realize that development. The only problem with this level is that a system of recording and notching-up of career progression may well be in place but the system and its results may well get out of synchrony with what is happening in and around the organization. In other words, changes will happen and the developmental framework is unable to respond to it.

Level 4

Management development policy and planning are closely linked to corporate planning. The organization actively clarifies its objectives and seeks to meet them through a management development policy which re-orients staff. For Burgoyne (op cit) this means 'it is possible for enough of the right people to be got into enough of the right roles with enough of the right skills quickly enough for the plan to work'.

The problem at this level is that the corporate plan may be non-implementable in management development terms. In other words, the people being developed are not 'malleable' to the demands of the corporate plan.

Level 5

At this level management development processes [a + IMD] relate closely to the development of the organization [b] in that the former influences and inputs into the latter as well as being part of the implemented output of strategic planning. This is achieved through involvement of managers in their collective future as well as their individual development. Human resource vision configures with marketing, technical and financial considerations. Here the organization 'demarcate[s] the contours of managerial feasibility that must surround any new venture and change' (Burgoyne, op cit).

Level 6
An extension of Level 5 with management development processes used to enhance the nature and quality of corporate policy-forming processes, as well as informing them and implementing them. Organizational learning takes place at the corporate level. 'When the company takes a risk, it does everything it can to maximise the learning from that initiative, whatever the business outcome' (Pedler *et al*, 1991).

Our experience is that organizational life is more messy and less 'organized' than is suggested in some of the above levels. Burgoyne took the view at the time of writing (1988) that a large number of organizations, perhaps the majority, were at Levels 1 and 2. Levels 3 and 4 describe the limits of best practice achieved with any consistency. Levels 5 and 6 existed as occasional achievements, 'often precariously achieved and lost and often only occurring in some relatively autonomous part of larger organisations'.

Levels 5 and 6 are, in the view of Pedler *et al* (1991), the levels where the organization may be at the stages of functioning as a 'Learning Company'. A learning company can only happen as a result of learning at the whole organizational level: 'A Learning Company is an organisation that facilitates the learning of all its members *and* continuously transforms itself' (emphasis in original). 'Company' is used to convey the convivial rather than to denote applicability only to the private sector.[1]

---

[1] Pedler *et al* (1991) find the term 'organization' mechanical, abstract and lifeless. We would agree but there is a risk that because the term 'company' is used to mean private sector profit-oriented organizations, we may well implicitly exclude public sector, community and voluntary organizations. Therefore, despite the abstract nature of the term 'organization', we have used it in this book because of its universality. But we also use the term to include the people who make it up. The organization is greater than the sum of its parts. The organization will have its particular climate, culture, myths and values. However, these characteristics are only realized through its people.

We have considered management development in three ways: as the manager's development; the systems of management development designed to meet particular individual manager needs; and the contribution to the development of the organization as a whole. In the following chapter we review how action learning can contribute to the three forms of management development.

Chapter 12

Using Action Learning for Management Development

How can action learning contribute toward the development of managers and the development of the organization? Action learning as a developmental process functions at a number of interrelated levels: the individual manager; as part of the repertoire of management development interventions; and as a contribution to the development of the organization itself. We will consider each of these, starting with the development of the individual manager, using the term 'manager' in both the senses outlined in the previous chapter: manager as 'everyone a manager' and managers with 'shaping' responsibilities for others.

Individual Manager Development

Our purpose in this section is to convey how participation in action learning can make a particular and significant contribution to the development of managers – the IMD in Figure 11.1. We recognize and do not underestimate the fact that managers will learn and develop informally in their work and lives (Mumford, 1989). We also recognize that managers may (or may not) have planned career development programmes and forms of structured interventions such as appraisals, career planning, coaching, mentoring and secondments. We distinguish action learning as a form of at-work development where the manager is directly utilizing the experience of work, from off-the-job forms of development such as obtaining qualifications via courses, such as an MBA.

Self-development is another strategy which an individual manager may take up, possibly with the encouragement of the organization. Pedlar *et al*

(1986) define self-development as: 'personal development, with the manager taking primary responsibility for her or his own learning and for choosing the means to achieve this'. Their guide was in part a response to the movement that wished to counter the idea that a manager's development was something that was 'done to' a manager, with the idea that managers could take control over their own learning and development with a resulting increase in effectiveness.

In action learning the manager is taking responsibility for her learning within the supportive framework of sets underwritten by the organization as part of the organization's system of management development.[1]

What are the potential benefits contributing to a manager's capacity to learn, develop and change by participating in a set? The significant benefits which we will consider below are: the development and enhancement of human relationships at work; effective approaches to learning and empowerment; ability to live with uncertainty and ambiguity; project management; and enhanced skills of facilitation.

Development and enhancement of human relationships at work

The relationships described below are developed through the deployment of a wide range of personal and interpersonal skills and abilities. Managers can enhance these through participation in action learning sets by working on relationships, working with others, reflecting on and moving to action outside the sets. Clarkson and Shaw (1992) clarify five aspects of relationships at work in organizations; they are set out in the box below.

Human relationships at work in organizations

- *The unfinished relationship* which carries the human need for dealing with the conflicts and hurts of the past, where the effects of past relationships are carried into the present, characterized by unrealistic fears and hopes which may or not correspond with the present.
- *The working alliance relationship* satisfies our need for 'doing' and competence where the relationship is between two or more people constructed round a shared task, which underpins much of what is

---

[1] However, in Chapter 7 we consider the use of self-facilitated sets which may be created by people without organizational support.

---

done, 'aspired to in organisations and frequently least achieved' (ibid).

- *The developmental relationship* where the focus is on our growth and developing the adult professional where the individual is provided with information, support and challenge to meet their contemporary development needs.
- *The personal relationship* carries our self needs and our need for recognition as unique individuals, involving trust, authenticity and affirmation often gained through shared tasks, experiences and values in the workplace.
- *The transpersonal relationship* carries our need for being, meaning and connection, the latter between individuals or groups. It is deeper than the relationships above and importantly extends beyond the people that any one individual knows or works with, but may include at its best some form of shared values across an organization.

Clarkson and Shaw specify the key skills needed when people are involved in each type of relationship. Whilst their purpose is relationship training in organizations, we will convey how some of those relationship skills may exist and be enhanced in the action learning context. The enhancement of relationship skills is underpinned by the use of the basic interaction skills considered in Chapters 9 and 10.

An important qualification needs to be made here. It is not the function of an action learning set to provide for needs that should be met elsewhere. In particular, it is not the place to provide for unfinished relationship needs whilst, nevertheless, recognizing their existence. It is important that set members and facilitators respect the right of the individual to meet these needs in their own time in appropriate settings of counselling or therapy.

The unfinished relationship

- A person's capacity to 'recognise, minimise, neutralise, rechannel energy from unfinished relationships issues into the here and now task' (ibid). An example may be where a set member has low self-esteem which emanates from distant, past relationships and which affects his effectiveness in dealing with colleagues. The safety and support of the set may enable him to address the feelings and try out new patterns of behaviour.
- By working in a set the manager may, through being able to receive

feedback as well as working on issues of significant personal relevance, develop self-awareness.

The working alliance relationship

- Team working skills are enhanced with the interpersonal and intra-personal skills and abilities that set members bring to the set. Managers, as set members, enhance and develop the key skills considered in Chapters 9 and 10 which are crucial to effective collaborative working outside the set. However, complementary to these skills are the skills of problem-solving, planning, goal setting, action and reflection which enable colleagues to effect tasks as well as get on with one another! Where organizations move toward less bureaucratic structures and control, to team- and project-based formats, these complementary skills become more important.
- Project team leading skills – frequently the core content work of set members is to progress projects. The project may be one where the set member is leading a team outside the set or one where the set itself is engaged in a project. The practice of sets engaging in reflection, planning, action and moving forward, followed by further reflection, enables set members to be more effective through the articulation of the process.

The developmental relationship

- Counselling and enabling skills are enhanced in the set. Managers are increasingly expected to employ the skills associated with counselling without, of course, taking on the professional role of counsellors who may have a very distinctive role in the organization. Examples of a manager using some basic counselling and enabling skills are appraisal and career progression. In the set, the skills addressed earlier and the role of facilitation (Chapter 6) which set members model and then assume, are important here in enhancing managers' awareness and abilities to 'empower the individual to take appropriate levels of responsibility in discovering how to develop themselves' (op cit).
- Mentoring, where the manager is using a particular relationship skill, is also enhanced through set practice in that the set member models good mentoring practice in enabling the presenter to work through her issues. Likewise, as presenter the set member gains understanding of what it is like on the receiving end of mentoring.

The personal relationship

- Interpersonal skills have already been considered above in the set context and in Chapters 9 and 10. The effect of the particular style of set meetings where one set member as presenter has her time with support and challenge from others in the set, alongside review by the set, means that the set members can consciously reflect upon their own and others' impact interpersonally within the set meetings and in their work. In the set meeting, members can 'develop their ability to offer one another collegial authenticity, sharing without burdening, and listening without caretaking' (ibid).

- Set members may, in the supportive environment of the set, be able to practise their personal effectiveness, ie, their ability to work with their affective side, their feelings and emotions, in a way that may be culturally inappropriate in the wider organization, and in the process widen their repertoire of behaviours beyond the set in seeking with others to bring about cultural change.

- By its nature the set is a group activity enabling set members to work on their group process skills. The positive and empowering nature of the action learning approach creates the climate for trying out, enhancing and developing interpersonal skills in the group setting.

- Set members may use some of their time in the set to work on and reflect upon the management of their personal boundaries, ie, the need to create personal relationships balanced with their role in the organization.

The transpersonal relationship

- A single action learning set cannot effect that connectedness between people across an organization. However, a set has the basis for linking the self with the whole represented by the set. When a set is effective each set member has a sense of the set being a whole of which they are an intrinsic part. That whole is also greater than the constituent members (and here we include the facilitator, if there is one). Set members, when sharing that feeling and value of a greater whole, tend to give a deeper worth to the meeting and working of the set and what they feel they gain from it.

- The connectedness *between* set members does not mean that there is necessarily a close personal relationship with set members outside the set meeting. It is simply that they share a feeling for the quality of connectedness that derives from the experience of the set. This is often in contrast to some of their other working relationships and their response to connectedness with others across the organization. We will refer to the issue of wholeness and the transpersonal in Chapter 14. Sets can thus give meaning to the transpersonal. The key which we will examine later in this chapter is how sets across an organization can contribute to the whole. Clarkson and Shaw capture our view: 'Organisations which pay no attention to the transpersonal are those without heart or spirit, that just 'go through the motions' (ibid).

The action learning experience and process can provide a model of the transpersonal by enabling managers to recognize, understand and feel what it is like. Managers are then more likely to be instigators elsewhere in the organization in combining with others to create the conditions for effective transpersonal relationships.

Approaches to learning and empowerment

The action learning process enables managers to develop and effect personal change for themselves and with others. The process creates the conditions for learning and for empowering the manager, as learner, to act and engage with the complexities of their work and roles.

We have already reviewed the contribution to understanding of the learning cycle as developed by Kolb (1984) which occurs in the set process in Chapter 2. Revans (1983) placed firmly in action learning the idea that learning, to be really effective, has to be about real problems in real life with real people. Action learning is distinctive in that the process 'stresses that it is as important that knowledge be able *to help one to act in a situation,* as it is to just explain or understand that situation' (Morgan and Ramirez, 1984, emphasis in original).

Much of our tradition of learning is about knowledge and understanding. Though important, knowledge and understanding are only parts of the action learning process. On their own they may make little difference to how a person may act differently in the world. Action learning, by being problem-related, means that the set member is an actor who learns to understand her situation, gain knowledge *and* generate action in a real context.

Another key element in learning via action learning is its social element. Individuals are not learning on their own – they are with others. The social aspect of learning is missing in Kolb's explanation but not in Revans' work or that of others including, for example, Morgan and Ramirez (op cit) and Handy (1991). Weil and McGill (1990), in explaining the diversity of experiential learning, extend its meaning to take in the personal *and* the social so that experiential learning, of which action learning is a good example, means:

the process whereby people, individually, and in association with others, engage in direct encounter and then *purposefully* reflect upon, validate, transform, give personal and social meaning to and seek to integrate the outcomes of these processes into new ways of knowing, being, acting and interacting in relation to their world' (Weil and McGill, 1990; emphasis in original).

Action learning promotes the above and encourages set members to take responsibility for their world which, with the social element of action learning, enables the set member as manager to empower herself. We all have a choice, even though we do not have full control over our lives, in how we respond to our world, passively or actively. Action learning enables people to consider that choice with a disposition toward actively interacting in the world. That stance can encourage and bring empowerment. That empowerment can be individual and social.

Another aspect of learning is the distinction between learning to solve a particular problem, referred to as single-loop learning, and learning that is learning about the way we learn to do such things, referred to as double-loop learning (Argyris and Schon, 1978). An example of single-loop learning would be where an organization's strategic plan reveals a potential increase in demand for a service which is responded to with a planned increase in trained staff, with consequential resources being committed to meet that demand. A double-loop approach to the revelation in the strategic plan would be to review different ways of responding to that demand other than the accepted response – in other words, to reframe the thinking beyond the 'more of', 'less of' approach. This means reframing the way in which we think about an issue by breaking out of existing norms. Given the need for organizations to be able to cope with uncertainty and inevitable change, the capacity of managers to think within single-loop learning may be an inappropriate response. Action learning sets can also provide the support of others who are 'outside' the problem to enable the set member to reframe the problem.

Action learning can provide the conditions for challenging the way we frame our understanding of problems. The enhanced ability to change our way of seeing the world means that we can have a wider appreciation of our world and with it greater possibilities as to how we choose to interact with that world. In that process is an empowering and active potential in contrast with taking our world as a fixed given, over which we have little or no room for manoeuvre.

Living with uncertainty and ambiguity

Linked to the need for the capacity to reframe our way of seeing the world is the loss of certainty. We now live in conditions of generic uncertainty. But growing up in a relatively certain world enables us to live and work in a mental frame that is similarly certain; thus our cognitive framework may be out of synchrony with the world around us.

The certainty framework may also inhibit learning because learning and change are inevitably about that which is unclear, uncertain, unsure. Handy (1991) refers to an attitude of mind that is a 'negative capability',

> which learners need to cultivate, to help them write off their mistakes as experience . . . We change by exploration not by tracing well-known paths . . . We start our learning with uncertainties and doubts, with questions to be resolved. We grow older wondering who we will be and what we will do . . . If we cannot live with these uncertainties we will not learn and change will always be an unpleasant surprise.

An aspect of that certainty in the past in Western traditions has been the tendency to create separateness and dichotomize things which do not have to be separate. Thinking and feeling, knowing and doing, subject and object, order and change have been separated and treated as separate. These dichotomies are breaking down. The process of action learning encourages participants, in working with real, live issues and problems to rise above these separations.

Dichotomous thinking is also about either–or, this or that, hard–soft, win–lose, leading and following, task–process, creativity and discipline, static and dynamic. Managers working effectively in the uncertainty business operate above these apparent opposites by framing issues that enable their meeting and merger. Underlying either–or thinking and behaviour can be a competitive dogmatism based on a simplistic way of seeing a problem and a solution which may also create win–lose conflict between the people involved. The set process can uncover the dichotomous thinking for what it is, lead to a more creative handling of ideas and help the manager, as set member, to work beyond the dichotomous.

Project management

We have reviewed how managers as set members progress projects with sets in Chapters 2, 4 and 5. Projects undertaken via action learning sets can have the following range of characteristics:

- Operational through to developmental for the manager
  - an operational project would be one that may be to do with making

more efficient and effective the way in which the manager currently undertakes her job. It should be noted that even here the project would have a conscious developmental impact on the manager because the set process builds in the articulation of the problem, planning, action, review and reflection, further planning and action in the cycle of learning as well as pursuit of the aims of the project.
- a more explicit developmental project where the manager is working on an issue or problem beyond their operational responsibilities, above the 'parapet' of their own operational experience. Here the content of the project as well as the process is intended to be developmental for the manager.
- Manager-inspired through to organizationally inspired
  - we have already reviewed in Chapter 3 the different approaches to the use of sets by organizations. Where the organization wishes to use sets to enable managers to define the project issues, problems and opportunities for manager development purposes, the manager is the determinant of the project, selected with some form of review required by the development manager responsible for creating the sets.
  - more commonly, where the organization takes a responsibility for initiating the projects, the negotiation determining the parameters and boundaries of the project will be between the manager undertaking the project with the support of the set, an external client for whom the project results are required and the set with whom the manager will test the feasibility of the project.
- Projects are real, involving real issues and problems of relevance to the organization
  - for significant potential developmental and learning impact, the manager takes responsibility for implementation of the project. The manager can reflect on the actual effects of setting in motion the planned and intended effects of a project. This has a higher risk potential than simply taking a project to recommendation stage; implementation carries a greater responsibility for the manager. The learning may on occasion be about what went wrong, what can I (we) learn from the mistakes that happened?

Skills of facilitation

Using an action learning methodology to progress the project, Morgan (1988) was involved in a major Canadian scheme examining the skills and competences that would be needed by managers and senior executives if organizations were to be able to work with 'the turbulence of the modern world.' This required:

- viewing people as a key resource and valuing knowledge, information, creativity, interpersonal skills and entrepreneurship;
- replacing organizational hierarchies with flatter, decentralized, self-organizing structures, in which facilitation, networking and remote management are crucial;
- developing contextual competences that help actors from different organizations across the environment and cultures work on shared problems through networking and the creation of alliances.

Flatter, more fluid and self-organizing structures mean that managers will need to initiate meetings, project teams, working groups and networks. With traditional forms of hierarchical and mechanistic organizations, managers are able to exercise authority and control more unilaterally and directively. In organizations using networking, control is more consensual, requiring managers to manage their relations with others. Moving and nudging toward agreement, negotiation and orchestration require a wider range of skills. Such interactions also require attention to balancing action-oriented tasks and processes with creativity. Effective facilitation skills can help to underpin some of these ways of working.

Morgan used forums of participants to explore the issues of the project and recognized that participants could hit 'major roadblocks that can easily overwhelm and reduce the energy of the group'. Facilitators needed to be aware of that possibility and adopt a style that allowed them to intervene in an active rather than a passive manner.

We have already examined the skills needed by the facilitator of sets in set meetings. We emphasized the importance of modelling effective practice in order that set members acquire and enhance facilitation skills themselves. Morgan cites four facilitation functions, each requiring special skills. We draw upon them here to emphasize the importance of these to the manager in a wide range of contexts. Their significance is the extent to which these functions and skills are developed and enhanced in the action learning process.

Morgan's skills of active facilitation (adapted from Morgan, 1988)

1. The need to *manage group process*
   - understanding the dynamics within the group
   - sustaining a task-related focus
   - managing time
   - knowing when to encourage speculation and creativity or a more disciplined integration of ideas
   - knowing when and how to end a particular session so that participants have a sense of optimism and energy for the next step in the process.

2. The need to adopt *a reflective, synthesizing approach to group discussion* that summarises and 'mirrors' issues back to the group, so that they are able to remember and integrate their ideas or deal with paradoxes that have been raised.

3. The need to make *interventions that 'frame' and 'reframe' the issues*, especially as a means of unblocking overheated or unproductive discussions or of energising excessively myopic or 'groupthink' discussions.

4. The need to make an *unobtrusive record* of the group discussion.

(Emphasis in original).

The facilitative functions here are obviously more appropriate in a group discussion format. However, Functions 1, 2 and 3 are also intrinsic to effective set processes in relation to maintaining the process of the set as a whole whilst working on the presenter's issues. Function 4 is also maintained by the facilitator or one of the set. Set members, as they progress in a set, take on these functions and skills so that all share in the process of facilitation.

Action Learning as Part of the Systems of Management Development

In this section we consider the systems of management development – the totality of development undertaken by the organization for its staff ([a] in Figure 11.1).

What contribution can action learning make to the provision of the systems of management development that should be designed to enhance managers' development?

Organizations survive, operate, and prosper in conditions of uncertainty and need to respond to that uncertainty. The quality of that response depends upon its managers, as important stakeholders. We have already defined managers very broadly. We contrasted their training and development and saw how their development, which belongs to them, is crucial to working with uncertainty. The development of groups of managers and the organization as a whole depended on that individual development.

To be effective, development undertaken for individual managers should *engage* them, give them *ownership*, *energize* and *empower* them in their development. For the supporting organization there should be *benefits* from and *value added* by that development, The developmental conditions should provide, 'the process of change, learning and development that affects how the person shapes and performs their tasks, roles and activities (Burgoyne, 1988).

In the previous chapter we used Burgoyne's (1988) model of levels of management development to convey, inter alia, the range and impact of the provision of type [a] management development in the last chapter. We recognize that organizations will be somewhere along that range. Any organization that wishes to use action learning as a part of its management development will want to ensure that other mechanisms are in place. Burgoyne (op cit) usefully defines the systems and processes which organizations can implement to move up the stepladder of management development incorporating that which occurs at lower levels:

1. Hard systems, ie those systems, procedures, rules and roles that are necessary to ensure that the organization contributes to the aspirations at each level. Examples include performance appraisal and review of career potential and development needs followed by an audit of the cumulative talent of the organization.
2. Soft systems involve the creation and maintenance of the attitude, culture, organizational and managerial style, ie the ethos and climate to make the aspirations at each level work and count. Without these the elements that make up 1 above will be aridly undertaken without commitment.
3. Collaborative career planning, ie a managed process of dialogue between every manager and the organization about career prospects and aspirations, skills and development needs. This is key for Burgoyne in making the

aspirations in levels 3, 4, and 5 happen. The planning creates good deals for both parties – the manager and the organization. The features of what is a negotiation between the parties are the opportunity for the manager to take stock of themselves and their work – what they are good at, their potential, their tapped and untapped abilities, what they want to do now and in the future, and their view of the organization, its policies and of their contribution to the organization and for their personal development. The results are negotiated but informed decisions at personal and corporate levels (Germaine and Burgoyne, 1984).

Utilizing action learning

We have emphasized some of the key developmental benefits which contribute to a manager's capacity to learn, develop and change by participating in a set:

- enhanced effectiveness in working with the range of relationships at work, including team working, developmental roles such as mentoring, working with and encouraging cultural and trans-personal change;
- capacity to learn, reframe and empower self and others;
- ability to live with uncertainty and ambiguity;
- enhanced capacity to undertake project management;
- developing skills of active facilitation which can be utilized to manage group processes.

These skills and attributes are over and above the basic but important skills gained in and from working in sets that are addressed in earlier chapters.

The combination of these skills and attributes are important for managers (and organizations) in developing 'a capacity for self-diagnosis and self-development on an ongoing basis, so that they become competent at being competent' (Morgan, 1988). We would add that development is also a shared experience to avoid the notion of the self-development happening in isolation.

In Chapter 3 we reviewed how sets could be used by an organization in terms of whether set members worked from the personal development end of the continuum or the externally negotiated project end. In essence, does the organization sponsor managers to join sets where the set members engage in a project with a direct pay-off for the organization? Or do they create sets to enable managers to take their own issues to the set with perhaps a move toward a project at a later stage?

Whichever approach is used, the organization can still require the review of a manager's learning and reflection to be built into the career development planning cycle. The line manager and participant manager can negotiate and agree the developmental targets and aspirations the manager is to aim for, prior to set membership. Following a cycle of set meetings the manager can take into the next career-planning meeting a review of what she has gained from the set in terms of personal development, changes in the way in which she manages and pay-offs for the organization.

We would not mechanistically prescribe a structure for permeating the organization with sets (because we are addressing readers from a wide variety of organizations) except to say that they can be employed with variety. We have reviewed some possibilities in Chapter 7. Below are some possibilities which meet a variety of management development needs:

- Project development needs of the organization and/or the manager as set member.
- Personal/management development needs of the manager in their operational role.
- Group projects undertaken by the whole set for a project on behalf of the organization.
- Sets to meet specific developmental needs of managers. Examples include:
  - mentoring sets. Here managers new to mentoring join a set to deal with the issues deriving from their role as mentors. Apart from the support, learning and emulatory ideas that mentors may acquire, the existence of such a set may help create some consistency of practice across the organization (Cameron *et al*, 1992);
  - developmental sets. In some organizations managers may have a purely developmental role, working on 'frontier' issues for the organization. Managers working on a diversity of projects form a set and provide an engine for each other in progressing the projects;
  - increasingly managers are working on distance learning programmes to enhance their development as managers and/or their specialist function if they have one. Here managers use sets to work through the open or distance learning packages and practice, as opposed to working on their own.
- Set adviser sets. Organizations building-in action learning as a significant part of their management development processes will wish to build in the facilitation process to reduce costs of external facilitators. More important, developing internal facilitators entrenches the ethos inherent in action learning into the organization, with accompanying cultural benefits. In

addition, it further enhances the facilitation skills necessary for managers (see the cascade effect in Chapter 7).

Manager-initiated sets

There are also organizations, or even parts of organizations at level 1 and beyond (Burgoyne, op cit), where manager development is natural and *laissez-faire*. Some organizations place importance on leaving managers to take responsibility for how they best use their time, part of which is for their development. This is true where the organization places significance upon the ethos of personal learning and development; higher education is a classic example. We would suggest that within such organizations, managers are able to create their own sets to foster their development either by creating self-facilitating sets or taking the initiative to persuade managers or staff developers to allocate resources to sponsor facilitated sets.

Action Learning and the Development of the Organization

We have stressed that the development of the organization is dependent upon the development of the individual manager which in turn is dependent upon the conscious systems of management development that are created. Each is interdependent, with action learning providing:

- a process and a vehicle for manager learning and development;
- a part of the systems of development for manager development;
- a process and a vehicle by which managers utilize their development and learning individually and collectively to engage in organizational learning.

With Burgoyne's model (Chapter 11) we are probably working beyond level 3 where management development systems exist but where they are out of synchrony with what is happening in and around the organization. Levels 4–6 increasingly link the systems of management development, and therefore manager development, to corporate strategies and development. At Burgoyne's most sophisticated levels the organization is learning and matching its development as a whole with that of its managers in tune with the directions of the organization, other stakeholders and what is happening within and around the areas of influence of the organization. The organization is developing as a learning company. As we have shown above, Burgoyne is aware that few organizations are beyond level 4, and levels 3 and 4 represent the limits of current best practice.

We think the model is useful as a mapping tool against which an organization and its key influencers can compare where they are with their possible aspirations. As a model it is difficult to take in the infinite variety of organizations. Despite the tendency to think of organizations as neat in form, structure and culture, they are more messy in reality. Given the trends outlined earlier, suggested by Handy, Morgan and others, organizations are going to become more diverse, decentralized and federal, with control more diffused.

If this is the case, then group and organizational learning may emerge from and within parts of the organization as well as the more coherent forms suggested by levels 4–6. Given this scenario, we can consider how action learning can influence group, sub-organizational and organizational learning.

We draw on Morgan and Ramirez (1984) and Morgan (1988) to underpin how action learning can support organizational learning by recourse to the law of requisite variety in cybernetics. For any system to adapt to its external environment, its internal controls and adaptive systems must incorporate the variety found in that environment. Reduce the variety inside and the system is unable to cope with variety outside. Therefore, project groups or planning teams should not filter out diversity. Select people to make for creativity for it thrives on the tension created by diversity, particularly where innovation and learning are required. Action learning processes and methods can provide the conditions for realizing innovation and learning through the diversity of its membership. Morgan and Ramirez (op cit) express the contribution of action learning succinctly:

> Whereas many decision-making procedures are variety-reducing in that they attempt to create a clear focus or decision domain by eliminating as much as possible, action learning seeks to create a situation that is variety-increasing. The outsider or non-expert who may only be tangentially linked to the way an issue is defined, may in the end have one of the most important ideas to contribute, by virtue of this distance and the fact that he or she is not immersed in taken-for-granted opinions.

Moreover, managers experienced in action learning who are able to embrace variety have the skills to deal with issues rather than take the first-sighted solution.

Organizational learning and cultural change

When action learning becomes an integrated management development activity across an organization and set member managers engage in 'reflective activism'[1] then at very straightforward levels the organization starts to engage in its own learning.

A simple example might be a manager who, on promotion, is expected to run meetings to effect some of the organization's business. The cultural 'code' here might be that those below a certain level of the organizational hierarchy do not run meetings; therefore our manager may be new to this role. He may well be unused to running meetings but will probably have been at meetings run by higher level managers. Easiest solution: emulate those who have done it in the past. However, our manager has been a reflective learner via sets and is not satisfied with this approach. He may also be daunted by the prospect and take the issue to his set. A trivial issue to take to a set? It depends on who is asking that question as well as the significance of the meetings being effective. Our manager may take the following questions to the set (or they may emerge from his interactions there):

- What is the purpose of the meetings?
- What do we want to achieve?
- What is the relationship between the meetings, outcomes and action?
- What does it mean to run one of these meetings?
- What is an effective way of running the meetings? Are there other ways of achieving the purposes for which meetings are called?
- Are the meetings really necessary or are they simply a matter of history?
- Do I need to run them?
- Who is at the meetings; not at them; needs to be?
- Of those who come, who contributes; who is silent; who dominates?
- Where is the energy? Is there any? How can it be generated to good effect?

These are just starters. They are not intended to immobilize our curious and reflective manager but as means of learning how to run meetings. Learning how to run meetings as they have been run in the past by others is necessary

---

[1] Morgan (1984) defines 'reflective activism' as the stance which encourages us (via action learning) to own the process by which we and others construct and sustain our worlds (Morgan uses the term 'reality' here), and by exploring those constructions we produce through reflection. 'Action learning encourages reflective activism that recognises that social change starts and ends with each and every one of us' (ibid).

– this could be said to be first-order learning. But this learning is within the confining limits of what has prevailed in the past. The manager acquires and learns the skills and knowledge necessary to do that which has been done before. Second-order learning (Bateson, 1973) means that our manager learns how to challenge existing assumptions and ways of doing things, so that some of the other questions above can be drawn across the mind in order to find ways of doing things which may be very different from those which prevailed prior to his promotion.

Moreover, second-order learning or thinking means that our manager engages in learning how to learn. The questioning, reflection, action and further questioning in collaboration with others in the set and outside is carried into all his work. The effect of this 'small' example is that the manager may bring about a significant change in the way that things are done – in effect be instrumental in bringing about a cultural change as well as achieving action via the changed ways of doing things.

Lift and translate one manager's ability to engage in second-order thinking across an organization and in the relation of the organization to its world, and we have the organization engaging in second-order thinking in relation to policy, operations, ideas and action – the components of a learning company (Pedler et al, 1991).

Our aim has been to convey, through very basic examples, how action learning can contribute to managers' development, be a part of the repertoire of the systems of management development and contribute to organizational learning. Action learning has been around for a long time. The process of action learning is in keeping with contemporary notions of development and learning and enables managers to work rigorously. Most important of all it is one of the ways in which managers can become conscious of the learning process which we believe is necessary for organizational learning.

Chapter 13

Action Learning in Higher Education

In this chapter we describe how action learning can be used in higher education. In management development, action learning has become well known and widely used; it is less so in other areas. Yet there is nothing about the process of action learning that would make it less useful in other professional areas. With the growth of interest in independent, flexible and student-centred learning comes a new impetus for teachers in higher education to look beyond their usual methods to investigate new ones and especially those which have a good reputation in other areas. We are not, however, making the claim that action learning will be useful to all courses or to all students. The approach is clearly one which requires a motivation on the part of the learner to develop through reflection on action. Nor are we saying that action learning will suit all teachers: the skills of facilitation are not the same as the skills of lecturing or leading seminars. Action learning does, however, offer a powerful method to those who wish to bring together the worlds of theory and practice. It offers a clear structure to those who see important links between education and the world within (personal development) and between learning and the world 'out there' (development of the material and interpersonal world). Action learning is also a process which can respond positively to the current trends in higher education.

Trends in Higher Education

Higher education in Britain is undergoing massive change. As we write, the polytechnics are becoming universities, students numbers are projected to rise by 30 per cent over the next decade, and students and employers alike are demanding more from the higher education system. It is no longer enough to educate the mind: universities are expected to produce graduates who are also conversant with information technology, able to work effectively in teams and have good oral and written presentation skills – and all this on a diminishing resource in real terms.

Larger class size

When the Robbins Report was written in 1963, a typical class size was 28 in a lecture or 10 in a laboratory class, and one-to-one tutorials were the norm for the majority of students. Typical class sizes in many institutions of higher education today are more like 80–100, with small group work being defined as 16–20 students. One-to-one tutorials are rare and unlikely to be routinely available, with the possible exception of research students. This is all 'old hat' for other countries. The United States and many mainland European countries have had a mass higher education system for years. The organiza-tion of these systems has a great deal to teach us about the possibilities for our own system and yet their systems often involve a very different structuring of the relationship between students and teachers than that typical in Britain. The danger in the speed of the increase of student numbers is that the system will not be able to adapt its own approach fast enough and universities may respond either by modelling themselves uncritically on systems which have proved that they can cope with mass higher education or by attempting to remain as they are currently and find that resources are stretched beyond acceptable limits.

It has been argued (Gibbs and Jenkins, 1992) that we must make a basic strategic choice between a system which highly controls and structures the student experience and a system which develops and relies on the independ-ence of the student as a learner (see Table 13.1). Both control and independence strategies can work well with larger classes but they require a different approach to teaching and learning and very different ways of investing in resources. Control strategies involve the teacher in pre-determining the objectives of a course and structuring the course very tightly around these, perhaps with the use of set texts and multiple-choice assignments. Independence strategies require the development of independ-ence in the students through investment in skills development in the early part of the course and in methods such as student-led seminars and peer assessment.

From the student's point of view, larger numbers can mean alienation, lack

Table 13.1 *Control and independence strategies* (Gibbs and Jenkins, 1992)

Problem areas resulting from large classes	Characteristic methods adopted	
	Control strategies	Independence strategies
1 Courses lack clear aims and objectives	Use of objectives Highly structured courses	Use of learning contracts Problem-based learning
2 Students lack knowledge about their progress	Objective testing Programmed instruction and CAL	Development of student judgement Self-assessment
3 Students lack advice on how to improve	Assignment attachment forms Automated tutorial feedback	Peer feedback and peer-assessment
4 Library resources cannot support wide reading	Use of set books Use of learning packages	Development of students' research skills More varied assignments
5 Tutors are unable to support independent study	Structured projects Lab guides	Group work Learning teams
6 Students lack the opportunity for discussion	Structured lectures Structured seminars and workshops	Student-led seminars Team assignments
7 Tutors are unable to cope with the variety of students	Pre-tests plus remedial material Self-paced study	Variety of support mechanisms Negotiated goals
8 Tutors are unable to motivate students	Frequent testing High failure rates	Learning contracts, problem-solving, group work

of personal attention and insecurity. Action learning, clearly within the independence strategy, offers an individual focus within a group process which can help to mitigate these problems.

Diversity in the student population

The student population now has a wider variety of age, previous experience, social and ethnic background and mode of study. Differences between older and younger students, between full- and part-time modes and many other differences both complicate and enrich the higher education scene. Welcome changes to the structure of the system have encouraged the mature adult learner and more emphasis on part-time study. We are a long way from a total system of life-long learning for all, supported by the formal higher and further education sector, but moves in this direction are being encouraged through various innovations such CATS points (Credit Accumulation and Transfer), APL (Accreditation of Prior Learning) and APEL (Accreditation of Prior Experiential Learning) and a growing number of Access and 'return to learn' courses. The implications for teachers are quite clear. We can no longer assume that the typical student in higher education is a white male, 18–20 years old with no family ties who will study full-time on one course at one institution for three years and leave with a previously specified degree. Some implications are:

- the need to negotiate the content of learning with the motivation and practical context of the learner in sharper focus;
- the use of more experiential and practical application methods of teaching and learning;
- the acknowledgement and use of the past experience of the learner;
- the need for flexible entry and exit points in programmes of study.

Action learning as part of higher education is an approach which acknowledges and works with this diversity. Action learning cannot be imposed on the learner and will thrive where there is a large degree of independence for the learner to choose their goals and, especially, how they will meet them. It is particularly appropriate for part-time study which is related to the work of the learner and it has the in-built ability to respond to changes in the circumstances and interests of participants.

Student-centred approaches to learning

The diversity in the student population can be matched by a move towards more student-centred approaches to teaching, providing programmes to meet learners' needs. In recent times teaching in higher education has involved a content of study that is specified in advance by the teacher who controls the pace and the method by which this content is learned and assessed. As we move towards more student-centred learning the control moves from the teacher to the student. Various processes such as learning contracts (described below) can help the teacher and the learner to guide action and learning through negotiating objectives and methods by which this learning will be achieved.

Increasingly it is possible to see features of the formal education system such as pace, structure and content being negotiated between the teacher and the learner. The trend is towards teaching and learning approaches such as the use of Open Learning packages which, while controlling the content, allow flexibility in pace of study, place of study and timing. Independent study degrees which are totally negotiable maximize this flexibility and also individually taper the content of the study. A student defines his own learning needs and a contract is drawn up by which he identifies resources he needs to support him in his learning, including the time of teaching staff.

The trend is also away from courses with a fixed cohort of students over fixed periods of time – modularity divides course content into smaller pieces allowing students more flexibility and choice in their study. It also allows increased efficiency in teaching areas of basic courses which can now be shared between different programmes of study; for instance, basic statistics can be taught to accountancy and engineering students at the same time.

'Roll on roll off' programmes of study allow students to begin a course at different times and, therefore, to finish at different times. This also allows greater scope for accreditation of prior learning, some of which will have been gained in the workplace through work-based training programmes or experiential learning. Here again, higher education institutions are moving towards the provision of programmes and awards and away from organizing and running set courses with pre-designed syllabi.

These new approaches to higher education provision are not without difficulties. Individualized programmes can be extremely costly to run, even with adequate support. Without adequate support and opportunity for discussion with peers and tutors, the institution of higher education is simply an award-conferring body and not an educational institution. Modularity, while increasing student choice, can damage the cohesion of a year group of students. Course membership becomes blurred with students less easily identifiable to their peers or to tutors. Isolation can be the negative result of a system which aims to maximize choice and minimize insularity. Without group support, an individualized study plan, using open learning as a resource, is nothing more than a correspondence course. While individual tutorials to support individualized programmes of study are very costly, action learning sets provide an individual focus with group support and therefore add value as well as being more cost effective.

Action learning is a student-centred process which guides learning at an individual level. It is a process which can be built around other types of provision so that it serves an integrating function. It is possible to imagine action learning sets where each participant is studying quite different modules but all come together to provide stimulus, motivation, support and challenge to their peers.

Links between higher education and industry

A further trend is towards more explicit links between industry and education. This has been growing through the sandwich placement courses, the new system of National Vocational Qualifications and various forms of 'in company' accreditation. These innovations blur further the distinction between education and training and between education and working life. Higher education is expected to provide graduates with transferable skills or capabilities of a general nature. Knowledge alongside skill will ensure capability and through experience this capability will produce competence. It is competence and not narrow subject knowledge that employers require of their staff (Stephenson and Weil, 1992).

Action learning has proved itself in supporting the development of organizations and the staff within them. As a link between higher education and industry it holds great promise as being a process that would be recognizable and acceptable to both. It is powerful in legitimizing a functional link between study and work for the participants through their work on action learning projects.

Action learning also provides an ideal forum for facilitation of learning to be a shared activity and not simply the preserve of the tutor. Participants in action learning sets learn to take responsibility for their own learning and they develop skill in supporting their peers. These skills, of listening, questioning, observation, giving feedback, etc are transferable to the world of employment, where graduates will be required to work independently and in teams.

Nevertheless, the cultures of the educational establishment and the business world remain distinct and for the learner this can be a stumbling block. Students want their learning to be relevant to the world of work but not narrowly so. A learner must expect more of their higher education than a reductionist training for employment. Needed alongside this emphasis on the relevant and useful are the concepts of 'learning to learn' and 'personal development'.

> . . . in the world of accelerating change (the knowledge explosion, the technological revolution, the information society) that we are entering, learning must be a

lifelong process if we are to avoid the catastrophe of human obsolescence. The single most important competence that people must possess to survive is the ability to learn – with or, more important, without a teacher (Knowles, 1990).

The imperative for higher education is to facilitate the development of students' ability to learn about the process of learning itself so that they become competent to manage and fulfil their future learning needs.

Education, in the true sense of the word, is essentially about development of the person. Knowledge and skill are sterile without the discernment to use both wisely. Higher education is failing in its most important function if it does not provide opportunities for its students to develop wisdom as they learn: the world, more than ever, requires this outmoded virtue. Higher education must safeguard its capacity to develop the whole person through learning by providing an environment that encourages and reward reflection. It would be a travesty if the enlightened encouragement of access for more students and the links between industry and education merely served to narrow the focus of higher education to the mere production of trained graduates. The real purpose of higher education is the development of individuals and the development of society. Higher education can develop both the pragmatic and philosophical, theory and practice; ensuring, meanwhile, that learners understand the process by which they may continue to learn. If it is to do this, approaches to learning and teaching must involve both the personal and intellectual development of the individual.

What is the Difference between More Traditional Teaching and Action Learning?

If traditional teaching is characterized (acknowledging this as not always being the case) as –

- didactic
- hierarchical control located in teacher
- dependent/passive student
- lecture/tutorial based
- cognitive bias

– what difference is there when action learning is used as a form of student learning?

Let us take an example where the tutor is introducing action learning to a group of students who will form action learning sets with the tutor as set adviser/facilitator, as a primary method of group learning on a course. Inevitably, the tutor will describe the approach, underlying values and procedures of action learning. Once that description is completed, the next stage is to do it so that students can begin to appreciate this process and way of learning. The tutor as facilitator will model the process. Once the students pick up, use and adopt the process the tutor facilitator can begin to relinquish the role of expert holding hierarchical control.

We examine how the tutor's role differs from her traditional role. Heron's (1989) three modes of facilitation are useful here (for more detail see Chapter 6). In the example above the tutor is initially in *hierarchical* mode as facilitator directing the process, exercising power over it and doing things *for* the group. She is even at this stage, however, modelling practice that will enable set members (students) to take on a more participatory active role – ideally from the first set meeting. We then move on to Heron's second mode – the *cooperative* mode. Here the facilitator shares her power over the learning process and dynamics of the group *with* the group. The group becomes more self-directive. The next mode beyond the cooperative is the *autonomous* mode. Here the facilitator respects the total autonomy of the set members. They are now on their *own way*, using the set to meet their needs as defined by them. The set becomes self-facilitating.

Note the differences between traditional forms of teaching/learning. Traditional forms tend to stay hierarchical in mode (through lecture, seminar, tutorial) with the student in a dependent relationship until the completion of the course and the results of the examinations. At another level, because the student has been continually on the receiving end of the hierarchical mode, she may continue to remain in that mode beyond the course, not having acquired the means and confidence to move to autonomy. Heron is suggesting that the hierarchical mode is appropriate at some times. In articulating the range of ways in which the facilitator or tutor may relate to a group of learners, Heron enables us to recognize the value base of our approaches to teaching and learning and that there is a range of ways of relating to learners. We can recognize the constraints we have worked under in the past and the liberation of moving, for the benefit of learners, through the modes to enable them to become autonomous learners.

How far learners move across the modes using action learning will depend upon the nature of its use. In this case also, the tutor is always likely to remain the one most versed in and knowledgeable about the course requirements so that the set members are likely to want to use the set adviser as a source of information about the course. A set which is incorporated into a course with a tutor providing continual support will not move into autonomous mode but can move into cooperative mode.

Another feature of traditional teaching/learning is the assumptions we make about the learner. Traditional forms tend to treat the learners as uniform in terms of knowledge, understanding motivation, commitment and background. As teachers we acknowledge these differences and the fact that they affect the students' work on the course but we have little alternative but to teach 'as if' these differences did not exist. This approach does not, however, treat learners as neutral, that is, all the same. The tutor will unwittingly convey an assumptive model of the student learner they are addressing. Yet the lecture theatre will be full of learners with a multiplicity of needs, concerns, dispositions and backgrounds, for many of whom the delivered lecture may not be conducive to their learning.

Action learning starts from a different place. A key feature of action learning (as an example of learner-centred learning) is the personal stance and background of the learner. The process, modelled by the facilitator, takes learners from where they are *coming from*. What differences are there in the set? How can these be acknowledged and celebrated for their individual benefit and for the set? Who is motivated to learn? Who isn't? How can a learner be enabled to work with their lack of motivation? How is it for the returner who has had a 15-year gap in their formal education? How is it for the recent school leaver from a Catholic community in Northern Ireland? How is it for the women in a minority on this engineering course? How can this group address these issues that meet the individual needs for each to their benefit and that of all the set members?

The other side of this is the personal stance and background of the facilitator (Salmon, in Weil and McGill, 1990). We as tutors cannot separate what we know from who we are and what and how we teach and enable learning. What we teach – the content – and how we enable learning is not 'out there', independent of the learner and teacher. Therefore the tutor, in modelling action learning, will also articulate where she is 'coming from'.

A further contribution of action learning for learners is the idea of learning through 'dialogue'. In this chapter we have stressed the importance of enabling learners to become self-managed and autonomous learners. This may suggest that learning is something that occurs in isolation or in a vacuum. We do not intend or recommend learning to be in a vacuum. Some learning is undertaken on our own but for us, learning means making sense of and changing personal meaning in a social context. For example, it is only by actually facilitating an action learning set that we can really learn how to do it, what it feels like and whether I like being a facilitator. For the learner as set member it is only by doing action learning that he really comes to 'know' action learning. Similarly, by communicating with others in the set the set member is able to give real personal meaning to his thoughts, ideas, feelings and actions. Freire (1972), expresses what we consider is crucial about 'dialogue':

> ... only through communication can human life hold meaning. The teacher's thinking is authenticated only by the authenticity of the student's thinking. The teacher cannot think for his students, nor can he impose his thought on them. Authentic thinking, thinking that is concerned with *reality*, does not take place in ivory tower isolation, but only in communication.

Action learning can help realize learning as 'dialogue'.

Structures for the Use of Action Learning in Higher Education

The process and content of learning in sets

Where action learning is used as the basic teaching and learning process there is usually the need to have other resources in support, to act as stimulation, introduce content, provide opportunities for group discussion and so on. It is important for us that in advocating action learning we are not misconstrued. Facilitating action learning sets is not the only thing a teacher needs to be able to do; quite the contrary. Action learning sets provide a strong basis upon which to build a variety of teaching and learning experiences. Action learning sets support the link between ideas and action. The action, for the most part, takes place outside the set and can be anything, including pursuing a particular content area through a specific mode of study. Ideas can be generated outside the set as well as within it. The function of the set is to enable set members to learn from the link between ideas and experience; to generalize from the past and to plan for the future. The process of action learning is something that has often been unfacilitated in higher education – it is the part of learning that has been left to chance in traditional teaching and learning environments.

In the examples of practice which follow we show a number of different types of programmes using action learning. These demonstrate a variety of other processes which run alongside the action learning sets, such as workshops, to cover aspects of the course content.

When the basis of a learning programme is action learning sets there is the ability to 'deliver' the content in many different ways, from a formal lecture programme through workshops to open learning materials and independent study. The content of courses that use the action learning process does not necessarily have to change at all. What changes is the way it is learned and the way that learning is used and becomes part of the person.

Tools for assessing action learning programmes

Assessment is often the most intransigent part of the higher education system. While teachers will experiment with different forms of small group teaching and new ways of packaging materials, there is often a worry that changing the assessment will irrevocably damage the standards that are so jealously guarded. The move to independent learning modes puts assessment in the spotlight as the control of the teacher is usually paramount. The logic of developing the learner as a learner, of developing the reflective practitioner and the competent graduate conflicts in logic, and in spirit, with an assessment system which is controlled, implemented and validated separately from the learner. Self and peer assessment help to develop the ability of the learner, not only to learn, but to test and evaluate the results of that learning (Brown and Dove, 1991).

An unseen exam paper where results are fed back baldly as a percentage, is obviously out of step with a learning philosophy built on reflection and feedback. Different mechanisms and procedures will judge the quality of learning in appropriate ways. Fortunately, as the examples below show, there is now an increasing range of precedents to show how action learning can be supported through an assessment process which is in line with its educational philosophy. It is important to note, however, that these assessment structures are built *on top of* action learning and are not essential to the 'correct' functioning of action learning. Rather, they are essential to the higher education system of conferring awards on graduates of courses and programmes of study. It would also be appropriate to have action learning as an unassessed part of a programme of study.

Learning contracts
Learning contracts are negotiated between the learner and the tutor or between peer learners to specify the outcomes in terms of learning that the student is aiming for. They usually take the form of a number of sections

answering the following questions: Where am I now (in relation to this subject)? Where do I want to be? How will I get there (including resources needed)? How will I know when I have been successful? What evidence will I provide so that I and others may judge my results? These contracts can be highly specified or more general and often proforma are used to help the student in writing out the contract. Contracts (or learning agreements) specify the resources a student needs in order to learn as well as what they will do to learn, ie, they can specify work for tutors as well as work for students. Students are also likely to take some time to construct the contract and may need to renegotiate at times throughout the learning programme. This is particularly important when an area is very new for the student as they are unlikely to know, from the beginning, what they need to know.

Example of a learning contract (in brief) taken from a course for teachers new to higher education

Where am I now?
I feel frightened before giving a lecture to a large audience.

Where do I want to be?
I want to feel confidence in my ability to cope with the large group and to be calm enough to read my notes and to control the pace and activities within the lecture. I don't want to feel sick before, during or afterwards.

How will I get there?
Sit in on colleagues' lectures and talk with them about what they do. Read about lecture technique and ideas for activities in lectures. Read about stress and how to control nerves. Try out the ideas I come up with slowly and at my own pace. Record the results in a diary. Reward myself regularly for working on it and for success when I feel less nervous. Review my progress in the set to help in doing all this.

How will I know when I have got there?
I will not feel so sick. The students may notice. My colleagues can tell me.

What evidence will I provide?
The diary of events and reflections.
The students' feedback at the end of the term.
Colleagues' descriptions of perceived change.
My self-report on how I am feeling at the end of all this.

> *How will the evidence be judged (criteria for assessment)?*
> How confident do I feel about lecturing to large groups?
> How improved are my physical symptoms before a lecture?
> How well does students' feedback reflects a good lecture style?

This example shows a type of contract which is based on a personal development relying a great deal on the reports from the individual. Self-assessment is obviously a crucial element in judging the success of the work done. A similar format could, however, be used to specify learning of a particular concept or understanding a particular process and could be described in terms that would be easily judged by a tutor with expert knowledge. Thus, in specifying the objective, the appropriate form for the evidence becomes clear. There must be a logical match between the objective and the evidence used for judging the outcome. Similarly, some objectives lend themselves to a result, ie, successfully completed or not, while other objectives will result in development which is unlikely to have an end point. In the example above, there is unlikely to be a time when nerves vanish completely – the question becomes one of when development is shown sufficiently for the individual to be said to have successfully fulfilled their learning contract. Where the contract is used for assessment on a course it is important that those who will undertake the assessment are clear about the nature of the evidence they will receive and their criteria for judging it.

Portfolios or learning logs
These are used to gather evidence to meet the contract. They are often a collection of materials and entries of a diverse nature gathered over the course and put together in some structured way to provide evidence of learning and development. Portfolios can be a useful way of collecting evidence of learning to meet a learning contract.

Profiles
A profile specifies what has been learned on a course. It can be a simple list of topics covered or a fuller description of learning outcomes. They are particularly useful for courses of independent study where the syllabus is not specified in course documentation. Profiles allow external people to see what was covered in the course of study undertaken by the student.

Journals
Journals or diaries capture the process of learning and the stages in a learner's development over the time of the programme or course. They can be valuable

as evidence to show learning and development at the end of the programme but they also act as a spur to regular reflection. Journals could form part of a portfolio.

Reflective document

This is a document written after the formal programme has ended which describes what has been learned. It can be used in tandem with project reports where the latter only reports the method of working, results and recommendations and does not adequately address what the learner has gained from doing the project. For example, in one course described below, the team project presentation was delivered to an audience which included the organizational client for the project and concentrated on the outcomes of the project and the recommendations for action. Although this presentation indicated learning in various areas of content the reflective document was much more specific in doing this and also covered the management and personal development that the students had undergone. They were also able to comment on their work as a team and on their individual learning.

Statements of relevance

These are written comments by the student on the relationship between input by the course tutors and their own learning with its practical application. They are reflective documents which draw out how the learner has made links between the general content of the workshop (or other input) and his or her own particular context. For example, on a course in Education the statement of relevance on the small group teaching workshop would comment on how the learner responded to the ideas, methods and discussions in the session and describe how the learner intends to change or develop their own teaching as a result.

Lessons log

This is a tool for evaluation of the course or programme by the tutors rather than the learner. It has been used successfully on a masters programme (AMDP, described below) as a regular way of learning from the experience of running workshops which feed directly into future workshops and into the running of the same workshop next year. It is simply a record of the feelings and ideas of the course team immediately after every workshop (and usually at intervals during the workshop). It feeds very well into monitoring and review reports for the course and is invaluable in planning.

These descriptions show how the assessment of action learning becomes an integral and important part of the process of learning rather than a summative external snapshot of attainment.

Issues for the Teacher Wishing to Develop Action Learning

Can any teacher be an action learning facilitator?

Yes, but the skills involved in action learning set facilitation are not the same as the skills of traditional teaching. Some teachers in higher education find that seminars turn into lectures because, they say, students won't discuss things, they haven't prepared adequately, etc. In order to be a set facilitator, I have to believe in the ability of the students to learn without my expert knowledge (they can get at that if they need to in another forum). Set facilitators are not teachers, they are facilitating the process of action learning.

In some cases the tutors who are working with action learning sets as facilitators are also teaching other parts of the course, acting as workshop tutors or supervisors or lecturers. In other cases the tutors specialize in the facilitation role and other tutors act as teachers of the content of the programme. This is the case with the DMS described below, although there is an overlap of roles for some people. This is a fairly new approach to higher education where speciality was formerly seen as being concerned with discipline. Now we have specialists in different teaching and learning methods and processes. Tutors who wish to use action learning may need to develop new skills. From our experience, the most important training a set facilitator can have is to have been a set member. To learn about it through doing it.

Can students working in teams become an action learning set?

Yes, but there are very important differences in being a team and being a set. The focus of a team is on the shared task and the skill mix and relationships within the team. Action learning can support reflection on the task and the team process but the action of doing the tasks takes place outside set meetings. If teams are working as sets they will usually need to define what type of meeting they are having, ie, if this is a set meeting, the process is a focus on the individual presenter's issue, but if this is a team meeting, the focus will be on the task and how it is going, or on the team and how they are performing. The difference is important. If, for example, a team member has an issue with relationships within the team, can the team, acting as a set, fully support that individual with their issue? Being intimately connected to the issue that the presenter is bringing to the set, and party to the action points decided at the end, can prove to be too many roles to handle. Conflict in teams will interfere in normal set process and indeed may prove to be the object of much of the work of the set. Where the team is clear about this and 'mature' enough as a group to handle the different processes side by side, then teams can be sets. The set facilitator's role in this case will be crucial in ensuring clarity with the set process.

How can I introduce action learning to students?

As with all teaching and learning processes the enthusiasm of the teacher will be an important factor. Chapter 8 describes a workshop that would be a useful induction programme for students new to action learning. As with all new methods of teaching and learning it is usually easier to introduce at the beginning rather than half way through a programme. Students who are used to group work will usually find the approach easy to adopt but some may find reflection in a group difficult at first.

How easily can I get a course using action learning validated?

Certainly this will be easier now than it once was because there are many precedents for courses run along action learning lines. Looking at other documentation helps, but also helpful are external examiners who have a working knowledge of the action learning process. Students who have experience of action learning are the best ambassadors for such courses and evaluations of programmes using action learning help to demonstrate its effectiveness.

Models for the Introduction of Action Learning into Higher Education

There are now quite a number of courses in higher education that use action learning as the main learning process. As one might expect, some of these are in the management development area. Indeed Pedler *et al* (1991) argue that 'The six-month management development programme which has a "start up module", monthly learning sets, occasional workshops and final workshop has almost reached the status of a new orthodoxy in some quarters'.

Increasingly, other professional areas are using action learning as a development tool and undergraduate programmes are seeing the potential of action learning for supporting project work. Here, we give a few examples from our own experience at the University of Brighton (formerly Brighton Polytechnic) where action learning has been put through its paces in a variety of courses.

Action learning to support research students

The Advanced Management Development Programme
The Advanced Management Development Programme (AMDP) provides a part-time programme supporting research and development for experienced managers in private and public sector organizations. It has two distinct parts: a first year leading to a postgraduate diploma in Business Research and two or more further years to support research towards the degree of MPhil or PhD. The course consists of residential workshops and monthly set meetings.

> The core philosophy of the AMDP can best be expressed in two premises:
> 1. Researching live business problems within organisations is a legitimate way of gaining a training in research.
> 2. A training in acquiring and analysing business information in managing real business problems is a vital form of management development at the end of the twentieth century. (From the course document, 1992).

This unusual programme provides a structure of support to enable managers to gain a research degree and to become effective internal consultants for their firms. Action learning is at the heart of the programme. The managers form action learning sets of between five and seven members early in their first year. They bring a work-based problem which forms the basis of their research project throughout the programme. The sets meet for a full day once a month throughout the three years. In addition to the sets, participants take compulsory workshops lasting between two and five days (three in the first year and one in each subsequent year). They also choose three (or more) optional weekend workshops on different research methods during their first year.

Research degrees are inevitably individualistic, as the learner is not on a course about what is already known so much as on a search for new knowledge. Action learning is most appropriate for this type of course since it provides group support for individuals in their research and yet the responsibility for development lies with the individual participant.

There are programmes elsewhere which aim to develop the manager at the same time as producing tangible results on real projects but this programme also develops the manager as researcher. A recent revalidation of the programme concluded that it was going beyond other similar courses by using research to develop the manager at the same time as the organization to which the manager belongs.

Examples of projects include:

- an action research project to develop a new marketing strategy for a medium sized printing firm;
- an investigation of the match between the espoused values of a large company and management actions as perceived by staff;
- the development of a strategy for European links for a large educational institution.

Action learning as a way of making a discipline-based management course more relevant to a company's training needs

The Diploma in Management Studies (Action Learning)
The DMS is a recognized programme of study for middle managers. Partly as a result of working closely with one particular firm, a new version of the DMS was launched in 1986 which used action learning to support projects. The company sponsored a large percentage of their middle managers on the programme and used the DMS as their main management development programme. The projects that the students do for their DMS work are chosen on the basis of importance to the company as well as being of interest to the student. Higher level managers acted as clients for the projects and contributed to the assessment of them at the end of the course.

In the first year of the course the students undertake individual projects which cover a range of content areas which are new to them. In the second year of the course the students undertake a group project which is at a strategic level and thus takes them beyond their current level of operation within the company. The action learning sets then act as a team as well as a set. The set's task is to focus on the individual's issue with regard to the group project. The team meets regularly to work on the project (without the facilitator) as well as having regular set meetings. The team works as a set but the set does not 'do the project': action takes place outside the set meeting and this action is sometimes a team meeting, eg, a meeting with the client to review the early findings or a meeting to construct a questionnaire.

The action learning sets negotiate and assess the learning contracts which specified the links between the projects and the content of the DMS syllabus. Introductions to the content areas are given in workshops and the tutors from these workshops act as resource advisers to the students as they undertake their projects.

One innovation within this structure which students found very valuable was the additional requirement for a *personal learning* contract. Here the action learning set enables each student to specify personal goals towards being a better manager. These are individualized and widely divergent, from improving a particular relationship with a work colleague to improving health through exercise. The power of the personal learning is in the fact that there is no client except the individual and the areas they choose reflect their own relationship with the job of being a manager. Action learning is thus a powerful process supporting both the task functions of the manager and the interpersonal and personal side of the job.

Action learning to support undergraduate project work

Action learning sets in BA Business Studies
In this course the action learning set is designed to cope with the larger intake of students and the consequent feelings of anonymity in students. The sets support the students in their project work by working on the issues that each individual student is currently facing with their projects. The course is taught otherwise in a traditional way with lectures and small group work. The sets have facilitators for some meetings and are self-facilitated at other times. The sets do not carry the assessment of the project and so, here, control remains with the teacher. The facilitators of the sets are not the course tutors for the content areas of the course and this helps the set to be separate from the course as a whole. Students are encouraged to use the set for their own issues, making the nature of the set process different from the rest of the course.

Action learning to support sandwich placements
On the sandwich degree, sets are also used to support the placement year when students are out in industry for part of their studies. Here the sets meet for students to share experiences and to reflect on their learning. The set members' action plan helps to enhance learning from the experience of the placement. The student also writes a diary-type report which is used for assessment for this year of the course. Students report real benefit from discussion of issues throughout the year with their peers and in the focus on learning that this brings.

Action learning as a way of developing the ability to work independently of the teacher

The MA Education

This new programme is a part-time course over two or three years for practising teachers. It is modular and includes run-on independent study lines where students concentrate on developing some aspect of their own professional practice. Action learning sets support these modules with fortnightly sets interspersed with 'critical study groups'. The 'critical study groups' meet without the tutor. Through this mixed pattern, students are encouraged to develop the process skills necessary to support each other in their study which leads on to dissertation work in the second year.

The students on this course have teaching skills as a basis of their professional expertise. The action learning sets are facilitated long enough to demonstrate the power of the individualized focus and the interpersonal skills required to enable the process to work. Thereafter students use the process in self-facilitated groups.

Action learning as support for continued professional development

The Certificate in Teaching and Learning in Higher Education

This is a course for teachers in higher education aimed mainly at an 'in house' group of new academic staff. The programme runs weekly for three hours, over one year. It consists of workshops on aspects of teaching and learning in higher education interspersed with fortnightly action learning sets. The participants draw up a learning contract to describe the skills they wish to develop over the year and they keep a reflective diary or learning log which includes evidence of work done against their contract. The sets agree these contracts and act as peer assessors of the learning log at the end of the year. Learning contracts are usually made up of three or four areas and the following examples show the type of objectives which have been included:

- To develop my ability to work with large lecture groups through learning how to use IT to produce handouts and overhead transparencies.
- To write a learning package to support a particular area of mechanical engineering.
- To develop my confidence so that I can increase the variety of small group teaching methods that will work with my students.
- To produce documentation for a new module on the combined sciences course.

- To develop a system of filing for student and course records that helps me manage my administration.
- To improve my relationships with colleagues so that I become integrated into the team and am able to champion the importance of my discipline area.

The rationale for the programme is that of developing the reflective practitioner (Schon, 1983). By this we mean that the teacher learns to question and evaluate her own practice and by reading about teaching and learning and through observation of her peers, develops her own practice. This is a process which becomes habit and remains part of the art of the teacher – as reflective practitioner. The sets enable each individual to draw together the theory and ideas from the workshops and the issues and problems of their own particular environment through an action-focused discussion of the teacher's individual situation. This action-based approach constantly reforms the view of learning that the teacher holds and over time builds her confidence in using a variety of methods and in adding her own innovations.

The results are often of much deeper significance than first anticipated by the participants. The action sets motivate and energize as well as solve problems and generate good ideas. Some have said that they do not think they would have survived their first year in teaching without their set. The stress and pressure of the first year of teaching can be mitigated by the understanding of peers and the safety of an objective group to which the teachers can bring their problems and in which they can generate action plans. Senior staff, who have found that their new colleagues become active and innovative teachers earlier in their careers, have recommended that the course becomes mandatory for new staff who have no previous teaching experience.

This course is an example of action learning used explicitly for staff development. There are many, less formal, ways that action learning could contribute to the development of staff in higher education.

Action Learning used for Staff Development in Higher Education

Action learning sets can be a central means of achieving staff development in higher education. There are a number of reasons why we advocate the use of action learning by staff. Most obviously, in order to enable student learners to acquire the skills to be set members and in time self-facilitate, staff need to enhance their understanding of the set process. By doing it we learn about it. This is particularly true of action learning where the process is so critical to its successful use. By forming sets for their own developmental purposes, staff will also enhance their skills as set facilitators.

Management development progresses out of staff development. As teaching and administrative staff in higher education take on responsibilities as their career progresses (eg, course leader, admissions tutor, placement adviser, faculty officer, head of department) action learning sets can be used as an 'in-house' form of continuous development.

Independent sets in the University of Brighton

Since 1987 there have been voluntary staff sets meeting in the Business School at Brighton. The first set worked over 12 months and when it came to a natural end the individuals decided to begin other sets to cascade their experience to others. This has worked to a good degree and almost half of the staff in the Business School have been or currently are part of an action learning set. Some sets have gone beyond the Business School to include other staff and some sets are now working on particular topics (eg, research), thus combining the power of individual issues with a specific focus. This has provided individuals with support for their work, increased the level of knowledge staff have of each other and the general issues in the school, and has enhanced the general level of empathy in the school.

Chapter 14

Action Learning: A Contribution to Individual, Organizational and Social Change

We have been conscious of writing for two main audiences: those readers for whom action learning is a familiar part of their working lives who wish to reflect upon and adapt its basic conditions to the circumstances in which they live and work; and those readers who are new or relatively new to action learning. One of our aims is to introduce action learning to the latter audience in a way which makes it accessible and de-mystifying. Another aim is to take some aspects of action learning forward which may have previously been understated or undeveloped.

What are the main features of the guide which, in our view, take action learning forward? They are:

- giving emphasis to process skills used in sets;
- focusing on personal and relationships development within and outside the action learning process;
- broadening action learning to include independent and self-facilitated sets;
- deepening the potential for action learning to be used for manager and organizational learning (Chapters 11 and 12);
- bringing and extending action learning into the learning process in higher education (Chapter 13);
- action learning as a sustainable and 'green' way of working, which we introduce in this final chapter.

We will develop some of the themes not considered earlier in the guide.

Process Skills

Detailed consideration of the processes which make for effective action learning, that is, how a set works best for the set as a whole and for each set member, have tended to be understated in the literature, and possibly the practice, partly because of the attention given to project and task orientations. We endorse Mumford (1991):

> The task is a constantly seductive feature of the total process. Learning about the process by which the task is achieved has been given a derisory amount of emphasis.

This led us to give attention to the skills required to enhance the process within the action learning set by considering the skills used by set members and facilitators (Chapters 4, 5, 6, 9 and 10). The use of skills, their enhancement and reflection upon their use in the set, represent an opportunity for set members to utilize them with more 'intention' in the set as well as in other contexts. Working with these skills in the set process deepens set members' use of these skills outside the set. The result is, ideally, to enhance their process skills and problem-solving effectiveness outside the set. As Morgan (1988) suggests:

> The special character of this approach [action learning] is that it generates knowledge through the design of a learning process that itself proves to be a means for approaching and 'solving' problems being addressed . . .

Instead of 'knowledge' we could insert 'skills'. Morgan borrows and adapts the famous phrase from Marshall McLuhan and concludes: 'In other words, the medium . . . is part of the message'. The medium of the action learning process is part of the message for learning and tackling problems elsewhere.

Personal Relationships Development and Empowerment

We have a threefold purpose in giving emphasis to the personal and relationships.

First, the understatement of process means there is a tendency to omit the significance of the personal interactions that will inevitably be a part of how a project or task is achieved and whether and how significant learning takes place.

Moreover, in Chapter 3 we show a continuum along which set members concentrate at one end on projects, and personally oriented development in organizations at the other. The emphasis to date has been on the sponsored project end of the continuum. At the personal end, a set member may choose to concentrate upon their development and/or work on their relationships with people in their working lives. We have aimed to add legitimacy to the ability of set members to work with their issues and problems. In organizational settings, working on these can have as much significance as projects.

Second, there is a recognition that personal and relationship skills and development have been understated in the management development and higher education fields. In the management development and organizational area, many problems faced by managers have two aspects: the technical, involving content, sometimes specialist knowledge – the cognitive element; and the social and emotional, requiring intra-personal and interpersonal skills – the affective element. Garratt (1987) stresses the need for an integration of the technical with the people side of learning in organizations, particularly organizations in the Western tradition. Writing of directors (but applying to managers) he asserts:

> An important part of developing the thinking processes of competent directors is getting them to handle the 'soft' areas of people and emotions as well as the 'hard' areas of analysis and judgement, and to believe that both are necessary to be effective.

For Garratt the need is to strike a balance between the two and that successful directing (and managing) and thinking is a key to organizational learning. Further, a low emphasis on the people and emotional side also leads to poor problem-solving. Garratt's quotes around 'soft' and 'hard' we take to be ironic as they should probably be reversed!

In higher education there has been a similar picture with the emphasis upon knowledge, content and the cognitive as opposed to the conative (doing) and affective sides of learners. We have already reviewed this in the previous chapter.

We believe the use of action learning, and with it, attention to the whole person, including the personal and emotional, can extend the learning and effectiveness of managers in organizations and teachers and student learners in higher education.

Third, there is a need to recognize difference and diversity among people. There is a positive benefit to individuals, groups and organizations in acknowledging people in terms of 'where they are coming from' and their wide-ranging life-cycle differences.

Until fairly recently, there has been a tendency to make assumptions in organizations about 'the way things are done around here'. Managers and staff have had to fit into implicit norms of behaviour that actually represented and reflected the power of those who ran organizations. Our society is still in transition in this respect – some organizations are endeavouring to acknowledge and work with difference, whilst other organizations are still living innocently with the assumptions of the past. This has recently been referred to as 'the power of innocence' (Baddeley and James, 1991):

> People's personal positions are arrived at and sustained by being in a group of people whose understanding of the world is similar to their own. Thus their position is both sustained by other group members ('That's the way the world is') or even attributed to the group ('If you're a manager this is what you think'). The last thing the fish discovers is water. Innocence derives its power through being comfortably and unreflectively surrounded by others of like mind. From this stance individuals cannot see themselves colluding with the larger flow of institutional direction and its consequences.

'This is the way things are done around here' is being replaced by the acknowledgement that those who created the world in which such a condition could prevail are having to reflect upon those norms and share power with those who previously did not share power with them. An obvious example is where women are increasingly finding but challenging the 'glass ceiling' above them and white men are discovering that the 'innocent' power they have held is untenable. That ceiling is, for some men, unwittingly applied at the personal level but is also institutionally discriminatory. A similar position applies in respect of race, disability, age and sexual orientation.

The key is to overcome the discriminatory practices without resorting to scapegoating or blaming those who have traditionally held power, as well as enabling opportunity for those who have not shared power. For both groups the result can be empowering and create a necessary pluralism.

> As the cloak of hegemony is discarded the individual can re-centre, . . . rediscover themselves and build their own connections, relationships and identity. This may involve a personal crisis but losing one's innocence need not entail an enduring loss of personal power (Baddeley and James, 1991).[1]

---

[1] The term 'hegemony' is for some a bit like 'culture' – 'When I hear the word "culture", I reach for my gun'! It can put people off. We simply take it to mean the prevailing plateau of power or ways of doing things with which most people live.

Let us not attribute the change necessary here to the use of action learning! What we can say is that action learning provides a process for managers in organizations to address and act on their personal position in work and with other people in relationships. The nature of action learning encourages the idea that what we learn (particularly at the fundamental level of how we see the world) does not have to be fixed and rigid. Rather it encourages us and gives us the skills to view uncertainty as something to be worked on and with rather than resisted – that we can each have a say in how we construct our realities.

Action learning also 'strives to be proactive and empowering' (Morgan and Ramirez, 1984). People have a choice as to whether they engage with the world and realize that reality in an active or passive manner. If they consciously choose to be active, by reflecting upon their experience and then acting so that they influence the nature of that experience, they can influence their reality. If they choose to be passive or fit in, then they are 'reacting to the construction of others' (ibid). Action learning encourages people to take responsibility for the way they relate to the world.

People may have the theoretical choice as to whether they enter actively into responding to their world and take some control over their lives. Whether and how people interact with their environments will depend on factors like their socio-economic position. But that interaction in the environment will also move forwards and backwards in terms of the person's personal sense of power in their environments. A significant contribution to our understanding has been the research undertaken by Belenky and colleagues (1986) researching the learning experiences of black and white women from different social and economic backgrounds embarking on higher education in colleges in the USA. They found that women moved forwards or backwards along a spiral referred to as 'ways of knowing'. These were influenced by their interactions with others in particular learning environments, and the ways in which they made sense of their experiences as learners (we are all learners in a variety of organizations – not just at college).

Belenky *et al* identified five categories of ways of knowing in relation to the spiral which also reflects a spiral of personal power in relation to learning:

> *silence*, a position in which women experience themselves as mindless and voiceless and subject to the whims of external authority; *received knowledge*, a perspective from which women conceive of themselves as capable of receiving, even reproducing, knowledge from the all-knowing external authorities but not capable of creating knowledge on their own; *subjective knowledge*, a perspective from which truth and knowledge are conceived of as personal, private, and subjectively known

or intuited; *procedural knowledge*, a position in which women are invested in learning and applying objective procedures for obtaining and communicating knowledge; and *constructed knowledge*, a position in which women view all knowledge as contextual, experience themselves as creators of knowledge, and value both subjective and objective strategies for knowing (Belenky *et al*, 1986). (Emphasis in original.)

Silence could be said to represent one end of the spiral where the effect of the learning environment is one of lack of power; at the other end there is constructed knowledge where women not only have their voice but are able to live, work and learn as constructors of knowledge – reality.

The most significant change we have seen as facilitators in action learning sets is when set members (women and men) have found their voice and realize that they can influence and transform the circumstances of their lives.

Independent and Self-facilitated Sets

Our intention has been to broaden the use of action learning beyond organizational confines. By 'independent' we mean that action learning sets are not sponsored by an organization as, say, part of the management development systems of the organization, or as part of a course in higher education. By 'self-facilitation' we mean that a set works without a set adviser. We have explored both forms in this guide – independent sets: Chapter 3, self-facilitated sets: Chapter 7.

It is possible for independent sets to have set advisers who may act in a voluntary or consultancy/paid capacity. Given our approach to facilitation we have argued that it is to the benefit of sets to move toward autonomy for two reasons: to prevent dependency and for set members to take on facilitation skills as they model those skills of the set adviser. Some independent sets may go straight into self-facilitation where there are, amongst the set, members with the skills to ensure the set works effectively. This guide is intended to be useful to support the initial stages of the set's life.

Put independent and self-facilitation skills together and we have a means of people coming together to work on their life issues as they each determine. Underlined by the value of voluntary commitment to a set, we have the ingredients for an empowering group of people.

It is a model that can be applied where people come together in voluntary organizations where the 'workers' are unpaid. It can also be applied to people in paid employment where the organization places a high value on self-organization, like higher education institutions and research bodies. In Chapter 7 we explored the ways in which this can work. The organization gets indirect or even direct pay-offs by encouraging such association to happen.

Action Learning as a Transformational and Sustainable Way of Working and Learning

So far in this chapter we have concentrated, in the main, on the empowerment of the individual. However, we cannot separate the individual from the social – the group, the organization, the community. Social change and development without individual transformation is ultimately totalitarian. Individual change without social change is difficult for the individual to maintain. Action learning is a form of cooperative and collaborative enquiry that links individuals to the group (the action learning set), to a range of groups outside the set and to organizations and the community. Morgan and Ramirez (1984) link action learning with individual and social transformation in an essentially democratic way:

> Action learning stresses that it is necessary to appreciate that human beings and their wider society are in one another in the most basic sense, and that effective social transformations must involve both. Action learning recognizes that effective change must start with the individual, but reverberate in its effects throughout a social system.

Action learning sets provide the milieu for personal transformation within a small group – social unit – an action learning set. If sets reflect in a small group, the whole of a social system, then action learning can spread its nature and effects throughout the social system as a whole.

Another related but unusual way of looking at action learning is the idea that it is a sustainable, 'green' or ecological form of learning and action. One of our sets recently included Shirley Ali Khan who was undertaking a major national project on 'The Greening of Polytechnics', using her action learning set at the University of Hertfordshire (formerly Hatfield Polytechnic) to support the progress of her project. Shirley found the action learning approach very relevant to the theme of her project and had this to say about action learning:

Shirley Ali Khan: Action learning is 'green'

My perception of action learning is that it is a process which enables individuals to make connections – connections within themselves; connections between themselves and their groups; connections between themselves and their homes and working communities; connections between themselves and the world.

Because the connections are personal, learning is always personally relevant as opposed to didactic learning which is often personally irrelevant. Relevant learning is quality learning.

An understanding of the interconnectedness and interrelatedness of all things is associated with the holistic way of viewing the world. The holistic view is an ecological view which leads to an understanding of people as a part of (as opposed to apart from) the environment. This view encourages the re-evaluation of the environment, since with it comes the realization that to abuse the environment is to abuse oneself. New personal values mean new personal responsibilities, including environmental responsibility.

Making connections is only part of the process – the understanding and knowledge part of learning – the subject being life. This life literacy includes environmental literacy. The number of connections made determines the level of life literacy and, in turn, the level of environmental literacy achieved.

The other parts of the process can be summarized in terms of developing life skills/competency and the translation of life and literacy and competency into action. In other words the process goes beyond holistic viewing to enabling people to be whole. Being whole would include being environmentally responsible. Wholeness can be both freeing and frightening.

We can consider action learning as an evolving eco-system. Mature eco-systems in nature are massively decentralized and based upon the principle of unity-in-diversity – the rain forests are a classic example. Immature eco-systems are massively centralized and compartmentalized and based upon the principle of unity-in-uniformity. Bureaucratic organizations are examples of immature eco-systems (Southgate, 1985). Action learning is a decentralized form of group consisting of persons across an organization or between organizations or a community. Action learning promotes unity-in-diversity because it is more likely to reflect the diversity of its 'community'. Instead of being variety-reducing in seeking solutions to problems, sets 'seek to create a situation that is variety-increasing'

Bureaucratic and hierarchical organizations tend to be alienating and energy-reducing. An example would be an organization in which what vision there is will be manifested from above in a hierarchical form to be imbibed by a docile work force who are supposed to harness their energies to that vision. Action learning sets are energy-creating and uniting. Organizations which engage in action learning mature and lose their dependency on traditional ways of organizing. Action learning is one of the processes that enable people to develop ownership for and invest energy in what they are doing.

Conclusion

In this guide one of our main endeavours has been to enhance the importance of the subject, the person and the personal in action learning. The purpose has been to redress the imbalance that has resulted in organizations giving priority to the objective, the detached 'out there' knowledge which became associated with management and with higher education. We have sought, as others are doing, (Weil and McGill, 1990) to (re)integrate subject and object, personal and 'out there', the thinking with the doing and the feelings, emotions and values. We have also endeavoured to relate working in action learning sets to the attention people give to what they implement between set meetings in order to be more effective and enterprising. To echo a recent view,

> The idea of an enterprise culture has been captured by certain politicians. However it is possible to liberate this concept from its selfish, self-centred overtones. It is possible to see the notion of being enterprising as synthesizing active, outgoing entrepreneurship with caring, supportive collaboration . . . We need to value the bottom line . . . *and* a concern for the human condition (Cunningham, 1990). (Emphasis in original.)

The integration of the subject – people – into the bottom line is not a soft option. Combined with reflective learning it is a tough option but one that we believe can challenge and change us and the organizations in which we may work.

Glossary

Facilitator
The person who guides the processes by which the set operates.

Presenter
The set member who is presenting their issues, problems and opportunities to the set.

Self-facilitated set
A set that operates without a facilitator where the set members assume the skills of the facilitator.

Set
The name given to a group that forms an action learning set. A set usually consists of four to seven people plus a facilitator.

Set adviser
Another name for a facilitator.

Bibliography

Ali Khan, S (1991) 'Action learning is green', a statement written for the authors.

Argyris, C and Schon, D (1978) *Organizational Learning: A Theory of Action Perspective*, Reading, MA: Addison-Wesley.

Baddeley, J and James, K (1991) 'The power of innocence: from politeness to politics', *Management Education and Development*, **22**, 2, pp. 106–18.

Bateson, G (1973) *Steps Towards an Ecology of Mind*, London: Paladin.

Belenky, M F, Clinchy, B M, Goldberger, N R and Tarule, J M (1986) *Women's Ways of Knowing: The Development of Self, Voice and Mind*, New York: Basic Books.

Bliss, E C (1976) *Getting Things Done: the ABCs of Time Management*, London: Futura.

Boydell, T, Leary, M, Megginson, D and Pedlar, M (1991) *Developing the Developers*, London: Association of Management Education and Development.

Brown, S and Dove, P (1991) *Self and Peer Assessment*, SCED booklet no 67, Standing Conference on Educational Development.

Burgoyne, J (1988) 'Management development for the individual *and* the organisation', *Personnel Management*, June, pp. 40–44.

Cameron, L, Jesser, P and Harvey, D (1992) 'Formal mentoring/action learning: transforming tomorrow today', Conference paper to 2nd Action Learning Congress on Action Learning, University of Queensland, Australia.

Clarkson, P and Shaw, P (1992) 'Human relationships at work in organisations', *Management Education and Development*, **23**, 1, pp. 18–29.

Cunningham, I (1990) 'Beyond modernity – is post-modernism relevant to management development?', *Management Education and Development*, **21**, 3, pp. 207–18.

Egan, G (1973) *Face to Face, The Small Group Experience and Interpersonal Growth*, Monterey, CA: Brookes/Cole.

Egan, G (1976) *Interpersonal Living, A Skills/Contract Approach to Human Relations Training in Groups*, Monterey, CA: Brooks/Cole.

Egan, G (1990) *The Skilled Helper: A Systematic Approach to Effective Helping*, Pacific Grove, CA: Brooks/Cole.

Freire, P (1972) *Pedagogy of the Oppressed*, Harmondsworth: Penguin.

Garratt, B (1987) *The Learning Organisation*, London: Fontana.

Germaine, C and Burgoyne, J (1984) 'Self-development and career planning: an exercise in mutual benefit', *Personnel Management*, April.

Gibbs, G and Jenkins, A (eds) (1992) *Teaching Large Classes in Higher Education: How to Maintain Quality with Reduced Resources*, London: Kogan Page.

Handy, C (1991) *The Age of Unreason* (2nd edn) London: Business Books.

Hawkins, P and Shohet, R (1989) *Supervision in the Helping Professions*, Milton Keynes: Open University Press.

Heron, J (1989) *The Facilitator's Handbook*, London: Kogan Page.

Jourard, S M (1971) *The Transparent Self*, New York: Van Nostrand Reinhold.

Kanter, R M (1981) *The Change Masters: Corporate Entrepreneurs at Work*, London: Allen & Unwin.

Kanter, R M (1989) *When Giants Learn to Dance*, London: Simon and Schuster.

Knowles, M (1990) 'Fostering competence in self-directed learning', in Smith, R M (ed.) *Learning to Learn Across the Lifespan*, Oxford: Jossey Bass.

Kolb, D (1984) *Experiential Learning*, Englewood Cliffs, NJ: Prentice-Hall.

Luft, J (1984) *Group Processes, An Introduction to Group Dynamics*, Mountain View, CA: Mayfield.

McGill, I, Segal-Horn, S, Bourner, T and Frost, P (1990) 'Action learning: a vehicle for personal and group experiential learning', in Weil, S W and McGill, I J (eds) *Making Sense of Experiential Learning*, Milton Keynes: Open University Press/ SRHE.

McLean, A and Marshall, J (1988) *Cultures at Work*, Luton: Local Government Training Board.

Morgan, G (1986) *Images of organization*, Newbury Park, CA: Sage.

Morgan, G (1988) *Riding the Waves of Change*, San Francisco, CA: Jossey-Bass.

Morgan, G and Ramirez, R (1984) 'Action learning: a holographic metaphor for guiding social change', *Human Relations*, **37**, pp. 1–28.

Mumford, A (1989) *Management Development: Strategies for Action*, London: Institute of Personnel Management.

Mumford, A (1991) 'Learning in action', *Personnel Management*, July, pp. 34–7.

Pedler, M, Burgoyne, J and Boydell, T (1986) *A Manager's Guide to Self-Development* (2nd edn.) London: McGraw-Hill.

Pedler, M, Burgoyne, J and Boydell, T (1991) *The Learning Company*, London: McGraw-Hill.

Peters, T (1989) *Thriving on Chaos* (3rd edn.) Basingstoke: Pan.

Randall, R and Southgate, J (1980) *Cooperative and Community Group Dynamics*, London: Barefoot Books.

Revans, R (1980) *Action Learning: New Techniques for Action Learning*, London: Blond and Briggs.

Revans, R (1983) *The ABC of Action Learning*, Bromley: Chartwell-Bratt.

Rogers, C R (1979) *Carl Rogers on Personal Power*, London: Constable.

Rogers, C R (1982) *On Becoming a Person*, London: Constable.

The Robbins Report (1963) London: HMSO.

Salmon, P (1990) 'Personal Stances in Learning', in Weil, S W and McGill, I J (eds) (1990) *Making Sense of Experiential Learning*, Milton Keynes: Open University Press/ SRHE.

Schon, D A (1983) *The Reflective Practitioner: How Professionals Think in Action*, New York: Basic Books.

Southgate, J (1985) *Community Counselling Circles*, London: Institute for Social Inventions.

Stephenson, J and Weil, S (eds) (1992) *Quality in Learning, a Capability Approach in Higher Education*, London: Kogan Page.

Weil, S W and McGill, I J (1990) (eds) *Making Sense of Experiential Learning*, Milton Keynes: Open University Press/SRHE.

Wilkins, A L (1983) 'Organizational stories as symbols which control the organization', in Pondy L, *et al* (eds) *Organizational Symbolism*, Greenwich, Ct: JAI.

Addresses

Ian McGill can be contacted at:
9 Nelson Terrace
LONDON N1 8DG
Tel: 071 250 3108

Liz Beaty can be contacted at:
Centre for Management Development
University of Brighton
Lewes Road
BRIGHTON BN2 4AT
Tel: 0273 600900

International Foundation for Action Learning is a charitable organization and an invaluable resource for the background to action learning and its continued development; useful for building up a network of contacts in the field. The contact is the Secretary, Krystyna Weinstein:
46 Carlton Road
LONDON SW14 7RJ
Tel: 081 878 7358

Index

DATE DUE	
F95	
JUL 1 2 1996	
AUG 0 1 1996	
GAYLORD	PRINTED IN U.S.A.